Leaving the Comfort Zone

The Adventure of a Lifetime

Olivier Van Herck & Zoë Agasi

gestalten

We completed our journey together. A seemingly impossible journey—almost laughably foolish. A journey by bicycle, sailboat, canoe, and on foot, skis, and skates. Slow, healthy, and sustainable. A journey of four years, three continents, and one ocean spanning 40,959 kilometers (25,452 miles)— longer than the length of the equator.

So little of our journey was planned out from the beginning. When we first conceived of the idea, we couldn't imagine what any given day would look or feel like. But our book chronicles how our idea became a goal, our goal became a journey, and how that journey has shaped our lives.

This book is part "how to" manual and part travelog. It includes practical information from the road combined with personal insights and travel tips. In it, we also share our personal ups and downs, our methods for overcoming adversity, and how we turned pitfalls into personal achievements.

We hope you enjoy reading about our journey, and that within these pages, you find some inspiration for your own dreams.

−Zoë and Olivier

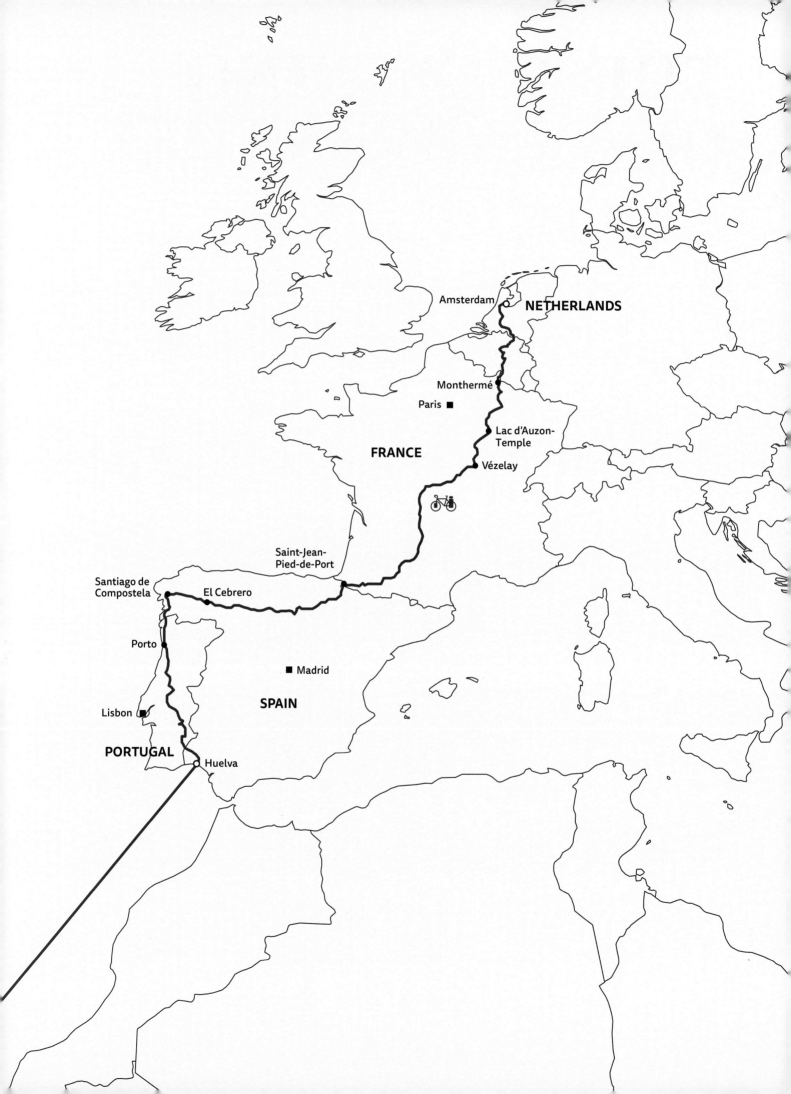

THE BEGINNING OF AN ADVENTURE

Cycling from the Netherlands to Portugal

We don't start out as world travelers or expert athletes in human-powered transportation. We don't have specific time frames or even the exact modes of transportation mapped out from the beginning. Our only concrete plan is to begin on our bikes, and we only decide that about two months before our start date.

We have next to no experience with this kind of travel, but that doesn't shake our resolve. We are confident that our voyage will take shape as we move, as we learn, as we become inspired, and as we grow. In essence, we have a good feel for the "why" we want to travel but want to allow the "how" to evolve on the road, waves, and snow.

A Shared Dream

How Our Journey Started

Olivier looks up from his computer screen and scans around the office. He has been working as a trainee in the Municipality of Rotterdam for six months now and is a youngster compared to his colleagues. He sees all his gray-haired coworkers typing diligently on their keyboards, occasionally sipping their coffee. He thinks about his colleague Ben. He was barely 63 years old and two years from retirement when he suddenly passed away. Ben was always talking about his plans once he finished working. In the end, he never got to fulfill a single one.

Olivier can't shake the thought. Why wait until my retirement to discover what I want? He jumps up, grabs his papers, and rushes to his bike. Olivier speeds through Rotterdam. He knows the way like the back of his hand. He usually switches up his route home, but today he takes the shortest. His brain is working overtime. He has made a choice, and he can't wait to tell Zoë. As fast as possible, he shoves his bike between all the overturned and abandoned bicycles outside their apartment, opens the door, and takes the stairs two at a time. His dream is now to travel the world; he has no plan for how, when, or even where, but he knows he must. Olivier and Zoë have traveled a small amount before but never anything on the scale that he has in mind.

Olivier's travel idea catches Zoë off guard. She feels conflicted and even jealous. She wants to be happy for him. More than that though, she wants to join him, but she has her own life and goals.

Zoë is completely focused on achieving her dream of becoming a rugby player for the Dutch National Rugby Team. She trains and competes six days a week. In the evenings, she tries to keep up with her studies in Industrial Product Design. She barely sees her friends, misses birthday parties, and has little time to spend with Olivier.

Zoë's dream becomes a reality when she makes the cut. But like all dreams, it's not without sacrifice. After two years of living together with Olivier in Rotterdam, she moves to Amsterdam to join the team while he continues to live and work in Rotterdam. But the seed of Olivier's idea continues to grow. In the meantime, Olivier supports Zoë's goal and sacrifices some of his own ambition. "You only get one chance to play for the Netherlands. That is our aim for now," Olivier tells Zoë. However, he continues saving as much money as possible with an eye on his long-term goal.

Then, Zoë's rugby team suffers a defeat that changes everything. It underperforms at the European Championships and loses its funding status. Salaries are cut, trainers are fired, and matches are from the schedule. It leaves Zoë with a choice: sacrifice even more to continue or follow another path. She is stubborn and has not yet fully achieved what she set out to do, but her heart is pulling her in a new direction. In the end, she knows her path is to follow her new dream of traveling around the world. Zoë makes up her mind on the day that Olivier hands in his resignation letter at work. She sees the opportunity for freedom, a life away from the stress of being a professional athlete. Almost instantly, doubt turns into motivation, uncertainty into enthusiasm, and jealousy into cooperation.

Even though we have the same passions, our personalities are very different. But our differences complement each other. Zoë likes Olivier's intellectual certainty. He thinks quickly, can remember everything, has a lot of general knowledge, works efficiently, is honest, and keeps his promises. It's exactly what Zoë needs. On the other hand, Olivier is reserved and thinks cuddling once a day is more than enough. Zoë is overflowing with emotions, while Olivier barely expresses his. Zoë is extroverted and social, and Olivier is introverted and reserved.

It is our similarities that shape our trip—our love for adventure, sport, competition, learning, and independence. We want to travel using human power, take local routes, be sustainable, learn languages, experience the unknown, stay fit, and travel without obligations. We want to feel, learn, discover, and understand the countries we explore.

We imagine our dream together and make space in our lives for our journey. Then, it is time to live it. The only thing that is lacking is a name.

What is WeLeaf?

WeLeaf is the name of our journey. It is a play on words between "we leave" and the "leaf" of a tree. The WeLeaf logo is a combination of a footstep and a leaf. The footstep represents slow travel by human power, and the leaf represents traveling with a low ecological footprint. Together, the dual images symbolize our commitment to sustainable, healthy, and conscious travel.

The WeLeaf identity helps us to reinforce our goals as we forge out on our long adventure to discover the world.

Bike Life

The First Meters

The moment has come. "Shall we?" says Zoë when everything is organized in our panniers. She peruses her place one last time, closes the front door, and tosses her key in the neighbor's mailbox. "Okay, that feels a bit strange," we say to each other. On the way down in the elevator, we are filled with both a sense of excitement and trepidation.

As pumped as we are about our upcoming adventure, the first meters feel oddly routine. We don't need maps or GPS as we cycle out of Amsterdam on autopilot. All the unknowns of the future don't feel quite so scary after all as we fall into the familiar rhythm of our turning pedals. There are panniers on either side of our legs, the bikes feel heavy, and sometimes seem to choose their own path, but otherwise, it feels like a Sunday ride in the park. Are we really leaving on a trip around the world?

We cling to a sense of familiarity for a little while longer. Pulling into the driveway of Zoë's parents in Breda at the beginning of our trip feels the same as always. Coming home, being home. This is where Zoë grew up, and her childhood is etched in the cobblestoned streets. We say goodbye to our friends and family on a farewell tour through the Netherlands and Belgium. From there on, we have no final destination and no idea where we will sleep each night. As much as we enjoy our prolonged send-off, we are both itching to forge out. We look forward to not having schedules or answers. It stimulates our curiosity and sense of adventure. We will find, invent, and create a new way of life ourselves.

Touring on a bike is wildly different than traveling by car. The distances covered per day are much shorter, and the usual tourist highlights are rarely ever the goal. Instead, simple things bring pleasure. A bakery for fresh baguettes, drinking water, and a lunch spot in the sun are all we seek. However, even this simple way of life brings new uncertainties. Are we allowed to have lunch on this bench in the churchyard? Can we use the road with a "PRIVATE" sign? Can we leave our bikes outside the supermarket? We aren't allowed to wild camp here—should we try anyway? What if the police come? While researching our trip, we read of adventurers camping in farmyards and churchyards, but now we are filled with doubt. We are faced with "firsts" every single day. Some hurdles we leap without trouble, others we clumsily fumble our way through.

On the first day in our unknown world, we are having lunch in a small village in the South of Belgium, and Olivier needs to go to the bathroom. "Just go over to that house, ring the bell, and ask if you can go," says Zoë, who thinks this is a perfectly reasonable request.

Olivier walks to the closest house but returns quickly. "Non" was the lady's angry answer. That was the first and last time we rang a doorbell for this reason.

We spent our first night in our tent at a campsite, but on our second, we want something more adventurous. On the map, we see an abbey with lots of land.

"Okay, now what?" says Olivier when the perfect lawn is inaccessible behind the gate.

We spot a woman going into the country house next to the abbey. After the bathroom incident, we feel uncomfortable asking a stranger for help.

"You have to ask her," Zoë whispers, thankful that her poor French lets her off the hook.

"We want to sleep in the abbey's yard, but the gate is locked. Do you know of another place where we can pitch our tent?" asks Olivier. The woman thinks for a long time but does not respond.

"Olivier, what is grass in French? We have to say we need grass," says Zoë. The woman sees our pointing fingers and then looks at her own property. "I also have grass; you can stay here."

We are proud of the success of our first little adventure. We have no idea how a world trip works, and as intimidating, exciting, and incomprehensible as it can feel, we are beginning to discover how *our* world trip will unfold. In the evening, we snuggle up close to each other in our tent in the yard. Satisfied, we fall asleep.

Routines

It's cold. Olivier wakes up as the first light hits the tent and illuminates his face. He reaches over and gently tickles Zoë's neck. "Uuuh, no, not yet" she moans. Her eyelashes are glued together, but as she pulls her head out of her sleeping bag, the bright light shines through her eyelids.

"Good morning honey," says Olivier chuckling. He wriggles out of his sleeping bag, deflates his mat, stuffs the sleeping bag into the sack, and within four minutes, he is standing outside the tent.

Now Zoë has the elbow room for her morning routine. Olivier always finishes quickly, but she prefers to wait a few minutes and enjoy the warmth of her sleeping bag a little longer. She arranges her clothes beside her, so she can get them on as quickly as possible. She then dresses in a flash and rubs herself vigorously to spread her body heat to her clothes. Once she has her jacket on, she can finally relax. Finally, Zoë rolls up her mat

Passing typical Dutch windmills on the first day of our trip. Colorful umbrellas cover the street in Namur, Belgium. The famous pilgrim's scallop leads the way to Santiago de Compostela, as seen here in the village of Vézelay in France (clockwise from top).

Pilgrim refuges and churches—like the Basilique Notre-Dame de l'Épine in northern France—
are the places that stamp pilgrim passports on the way to Santiago de Compostela.

neatly and arranges everything in the panniers in exactly the right place. Then she is ready to roll.

Gradually, all our stuff has its rightful place. This structure brings security—to know which bag to dig into to find something and to close the bag each morning knowing we haven't forgotten anything.

Whether it is riding around the world or doing the weekly shopping, humans are wired to find rhythm. Rhythm lets us organize, organization brings efficiency, and efficiency helps us reach our goals. Rhythmically, we do the same things every day: we get up, get on our bikes, have lunch, continue cycling, and find a place to sleep. By 7 p.m., we are comfortably in our sleeping bags cradling our laptops to record our daily statistics. Every day we keep track of what we spend, where we sleep, how many kilometers we have covered, and the time it takes us.

Sometimes it feels like our lives on the bikes have been reduced to a schedule. We set off on this journey to find freedom, but there are days when it feels like we are so caught up in quantifying our "freedom" that our journey risks being reduced to numbers. When we start to feel this way, we consciously change our routine—from small things (like sleeping on opposite sides of the tent) to more radical things (like taking days off or changing routes). Each change revitalizes our enthusiasm.

In the end, we strike a happy medium with our routine. The structure provides comfort when we need it and gives us a literal and metaphorical route map to reach our goals. While having the freedom to mix it up allows us to feel adventurous and free.

The village of Rocamadour has attracted pilgrims for centuries. As a child, Olivier was here with his parents and was impressed to see pilgrims getting up the stairs on their knees. When we knock on the door of a church to get pilgrim stamps, the priest takes our hands and sings us a pilgrim song.

Nature and history alternate while heading south on the Camino de Santiago pilgrimage route. The famous Pont Valentré in the city of Cahors (above).

We Are Pilgrims

Riding Back in Time on the Camino de Santiago

It is October, and we have crossed Belgium and are in central France. Vézelay is the first real pilgrim town along the Camino de Santiago and a milestone on this part of our journey. As we approach the entrance gates of the cathedral, a dazzling glimmer of gold catches our eye. Like a sparkling nugget among the cobblestones, we see the first shining scallop shell—the symbol of the pilgrimage. This ubiquitous symbol will become a familiar sight over the next 1,000 kilometers (600 miles).

It's late in the season, so Sister Gisèle of Centre Madeleine says that there probably won't be any other pilgrims when suddenly an old man is standing in the doorway. He is mostly bald, with a small wound on the top of his head and a full white beard. He is dressed in a thick wool sweater with some kind of riding breeches underneath. Despite the autumnal weather outside, he isn't wearing any shoes. Upon hearing Zoë's name, he enthusiastically hollers out the name of Saint Zoe and launches into a detailed tale about her. He alternates between a low whisper and a bellowing shout. He enquires about Olivier's name, but it doesn't interest him. Then, he calmly sits down and enjoys a mug of hot chocolate.

The barefoot man returns that evening, this time dressed in a white robe that comes just above his knees as if he has just walked out of a surgery in the hospital. He asks if we want to see his house. Curious and a little apprehensive, we follow him outside. "Do you always walk barefoot?" asks Zoë as she zips up her warm jacket. "Yes, and I prefer not to wear clothes at all. At home, I'm always naked. But you can't do that on the street."

We walk along the old city walls through the mud, and he proudly tells us that he bathed two days ago—just like the birds do. This makes him happy, and he does his best bird impression. Outside the city walls, there is a tiny house. Inside, it is warm and cozy. There is a couch, two chairs, and large posters of the movie *Casino* and The Beatles on the wall. There is a half-eaten bowl of rice, dry cookies, and some papers on the table. Other than that, there aren't many things. He asks if we would like a hot drink, and we smile as he begins to make tea.

When the water is on the stove, he settles on the couch in front of us. We ask him if he has always been a pilgrim, and he tells us about a monastery in Paris where he lived and sang songs. He takes out a booklet with a picture of the old monastery from the cupboard. Then he takes out a sheet of paper and writes down a song. Hunched over deeply, he tries to shake the last English words out of his brain. With a little help from us, he gets the text on paper. He sings the song in English for us and then repeats it in Russian and French. He then signs the text with two crosses, gives it to us, kisses us both on the cheek twice, and wishes us a good pilgrimage.

The barefoot man epitomizes our unique experience on the Camino de Santiago. Along the way, we are cheered and encouraged. Some people grab our arms and sing us pilgrim songs. We are made to feel special because priests and nuns empathize wholeheartedly with us despite our conviction being rooted in adventure rather than religion. We respect each other's beliefs and find more in common than separates us.

An uphill battle

How many hills?" asks Zoë. Olivier knows every peak, descent, climb, and valley from the route profile on the GPS device on his handlebars. He is the live commentator when we are on the road and knows exactly what is coming. "Three climbs—two short ones and one long climb."

He knows she doesn't want to know more. Zoë is a strong climber, but she doesn't like the word "about." Certainly not when Olivier says "about" 5 kilometers (3 miles) until the end. As soon as she knows she's almost done, she starts counting every turn of the pedal. They seem to get heavier by the moment. For Zoë, "about" finished is when she sees the finish line or even when she's crossed it. However, she likes knowing roughly what's in store for her before focusing her thoughts on other things.

We are both climbing specialists or *grimpeur* as the French say. We prefer the mountains to the plains. We enjoy the physical challenge of each climb but understand that not everybody feels that way. In Spain, Simon, Olivier's brother, joins us for three weeks on the way to Santiago de Compostela. The road splits, and we are faced with a route dilemma. Should we opt for the shortcut via a murderous climb in the next section or detour 15 kilometers (9½ miles) to avoid it? A quick calculation shows that we can cycle an hour longer over the climb and still be faster than the detour. Moreover, we relish the idea of sweating, huffing, and puffing, but aren't sure if Simon shares our enthusiasm for the vertical. With a mixture of doubt and motivation, we decide on the climb. No sooner than we have muttered the words, "This is doable," do we see what looms around the corner.

"Ouch." Ahead of us begins a vertical climb averaging 11 percent—steeper than the famous Alpe d'Huez. We tacitly

see it as a competition to draw extra strength. None of us wants to give up and face the ignominy of putting a foot down. Simon finds energy in the beauty of the surroundings, distracting himself from the toil. Zoë embraces the pain and enjoys riding on the edge of complete exhaustion. With eyes fixed on the road and with controlled breathing, she repeats the mantra "keep cycling, keep going." Whereas Olivier, makes mental goals on the GPS trace in front of him, carefully marking off each turn and steep ramp. Now and then, he treats himself to a backward glance to marvel at how much he has already climbed. The last time he looks back, he knows he has won the competition. Much to the frustration of Zoë, who seemed to be headed for victory until past the halfway point, Olivier reaches the summit first. He waits for the others at the top with a can of Coke as his reward.

We don't always climb with such pleasure. There are those days with countless small climbs, which mentally exhaust us. On these rollercoaster roads, our heavy bikes plummet down the descents like stones but come to a near standstill as soon as gravity is against us. From the highest gear, we click our shifters until we reach the easiest cogs. On the steepest of climbs, we click again and again, willing our bikes to grow another gear. Instead, we just pedal that little bit harder to keep moving. On the very hardest days, we keep checking our tires for punctures—any excuse to justify how slowly we are moving and how hard it feels to keep going. There are never any punctures.

Regardless of how relentless the climb can feel on the way up, the reward at the top always makes it worth the effort. We never grow tired of that sense of accomplishment.

Striking a balance

A few days before Santiago de Compostela, our stubbornness nearly prevents us from enjoying one of our most memorable experiences. We have a destination in mind for the day. There is a pilgrim hostel exactly 80 kilometers (50 miles) away. 5 kilometers (3 miles) before our intended destination, we pass a cozy hostel, which would be ideal for our upcoming planned rest day.

We are conflicted. We are tired, this place is beautiful—and we aren't certain what the next hostel will be like. But we haven't completed our distance for the day. We haven't earned the right to stop yet. We continue but keep arguing. Deep down, we all wanted to stay, but our stubbornness and a sense of pride prevented each of us from trying to convince the others. In the end, Simon finally puts his foot down. He makes the point that by the time we return, we will have covered our target distance for the day. We are reminded of our self-imposed rules and the value of breaking away from routine from time to time. We turn back, and as soon as we arrive, we instantly know we have made the right decision.

The next day there will be an annual village festival, and everyone is welcome. There is going to be a huge bonfire and enough food for the whole village. The next evening, we are eating roasted chestnuts and chatting with locals around the fire. No stubbornness can compete with that.

Galicia is one big mountainous forest crisscrossed with well laid out asphalt roads. It is full of tall eucalyptus trees, with the occasional oak tree peeping through. It is so quiet that we almost feel deaf. It feels like cycling back in time to a simpler way of life.

The Camino Frances, the most traditional of all pilgrim routes to Santiago de Compostela, takes us through vineyards in northern Spain.
It's early November, and all the vines have turned yellow, orange, and red (opposite).

Every 10 kilometers (6 miles) a village of a handful of houses pops up. The ancient land divisions of moss-covered walls divide the yards of each house. The small abodes are built of natural stone and accompanied by strange, small structures built on round, cut stones. These *horreos* are old storage houses for grain and corn, built so that mice cannot get in. We pass old women with baskets on their heads, others peeling potatoes, or hanging laundry outside while old men with axes and hoes putter around their land. We break the silence to greet an old lady with a stick in her hand next to two scrawny cows. She looks up and waves, moving so slowly that we have almost left the village by the time her gesture is complete.

Upon reaching the outskirts of the ancient city of Santiago de Compostela, our GPS guides us via a back gate through the medieval city walls. Suddenly, we are standing in front of the impressive cathedral that marks the end of this chapter of our journey. We pick up our certificate at the pilgrim's office—an award for our efforts.

The route to Compostela was beautiful, and we can't believe that we are standing here. We tie a scallop shell memento to our handlebar bags and set our sights on Portugal.

All the way to Santiago de Compostela, churches have been our favorite lunch spots and good places to observe local life. We arrive at the right moment for the annual village festival in Santa Catalina de Somoza (opposite).

Stories of Travelers

Our Search for a Sailboat in Portugal

A small lawn opposite a church in Portugal seems like the perfect place to pitch our tent. There are a few people by the church who are just about to get into their car. "Is the pastor here?" we try in Spanish, to which an old man steps forward. We don't speak Portuguese and can't quite explain what we're looking for. With gestures, we try to make clear that we would like to pitch our tent under the tree in the courtyard. Fortunately, our fully packed bicycles speak volumes. The rest of the group joins the conversation.

"In the tent, it is way too cold. They can sleep inside the church," the pastor seems to say and motions us over. "There is electricity and water. This is much better than outside," says the pastor pointing to everything and opening the tap. For us, this upgrade is like a luxury hotel.

"It's still cold here. Doesn't the heating work?" asks the mother of the family that joined us inside. They are deep in discussion, but we don't understand a word of Portuguese.

Suddenly, the daughter starts speaking to us in fluent English. "My mother invites you to our house." The daughter says that she is shy about her English and that her mother doesn't speak English at all. We follow their car, full of adrenaline. "We just got invited to someone's house!" Zoë says with a smile from ear to ear.

In the cozy living room, there is a TV, a large couch, and a Christmas tree. It could easily be the Netherlands. We are invited to sit at the kitchen table and are given sandwiches and soup. The daughter, Ana, is chatting away and the son, Tiago, also joins us. Both are fluent in English, and we talk to each other like best friends. One dish after another appears on the table and mom makes sure we aren't lacking anything. Ana translates everything we say, and they ask us questions. In the evening, we all watch Portuguese television and take a picture with the whole family by the Christmas tree. They tell us that they will hang it between the family photos next to the TV.

Porto is a city with thousands of steps and alleys. Its lifeline, the Douro River, runs through the center. Next to the river are large porthouses where, in the old days, the famous sweet red wine was brought to market and exported all over Europe.

Later Ana shows us our room. "But this is your parents' room! We have mats and can sleep on the floor," we say bewildered.

"My mother will never accept that, so get into bed quickly," Ana laughs cheerfully.

When we are in bed, we look at each other and know that our trip and our lives will never be the same after tonight. We've heard stories of travelers being invited to stay with families, often in far away and unknown countries. We thought the modern world had changed, but our adopted family showed us that kindness endures. The kitchen table becomes our favorite place throughout the rest of our journey.

"A gift from my mother, to say thank you, and for a little snack along the way," says Ana the next morning with an envelope in hand. We have already received so much that we cannot possibly accept this, but Ana won't take no for an answer. "Please, accept it," she says.

That evening we read a post from Ana on Facebook. It's our family photo with the caption "Christmas came early this year."

In the harbor of Porto, we are taken back in time. Old men repair fishing nets in wooden shacks, while women wash clothes by hand in old bathhouses.

Warmshowers

Our next destination—Porto—looms large in our minds. It will mark the end of our cycling for a while, and we will start looking for a boat to begin the second leg of our journey. However, first we have to reach the coast. We decide to take the Portuguese pilgrim route to the coast.

Along the way, we meet a French cyclist trying to lift her bike over a barrier. We assume she'll also be sleeping in pilgrim hostels and suggest we cycle together. "I'm going to a Warmshower this evening," says Marlène. "A warm shower?" asks Zoë.

Marlène explains that the Warmshowers Community is a free worldwide hospitality exchange for touring cyclists who enjoy helping each other. A new world opens for us. Intrigued, that evening we create a profile on the website and write a message to a Warmshowers host in Porto.

Two days later, we are standing in front of Rui's door. He sends us a message explaining he's at work and won't be home when we arrive but tells us where the key is hidden and to make ourselves at home. Taken back by his trust, we put the key in the lock. Despite the permission, it feels like we are breaking into a stranger's house. Just before we open the door, we hear voices, and the door flies open by itself. Suddenly we're inside a small kitchen filled with people. A boy says hello with a German-English accent and leaves. Amazed, we look around. Two American ladies are loudly present, a somewhat quiet boy

stands in a corner, and a barefoot hippie is busy with herbs. Mattresses, beds, and sleeping mats take up every square foot of the apartment.

Rui is a host on a similar website—Couchsurfing—as well. He says "yes" to every traveler who knocks on his door. With Porto being one of Portugal's tourist hotspots, he is rarely alone. Tonight, 17 people are sleeping in his apartment. Rui himself finds a free spot on the floor when he comes home at night and rolls out his mat there. He traveled around the world for six years himself and this is his way of paying back hospitality.

The next day, we wrap up against the rain and head down to the quay. There are two hundred boats in the harbor. One of them must be crossing the ocean, we think. But the receptionist quells our hopes. "All these boats winter in the harbor. Sailors who cross the ocean are long gone." A sense of fear and anxiety overwhelms us.

Dealing with the unknown

- We don't need to know everything to take the first step.
- Fear arises when we don't know what's coming, or we feel we have no control. The cure for fear lies in its opposite: confidence. By gathering knowledge and building experience, we gain confidence, and our fear diminishes.
- We don't always have to have a plan. Sometimes we just need to breathe, trust, let go, and see what happens.

Portugal's interior enchants us. White villages sit atop hills, and the landscape is full of olive trees and cork oaks. The bark of the oaks is harvested every ten years and used for the production of wine corks and cork flooring.

What to Consider before Hitting the Road

How to Plan, What to Bring, and Tips on Traveling Together

Our bikes

There we are—two aspiring world cyclists in a bicycle shop in Rotterdam. We stare at the different models until we see the price tags. There isn't a single bicycle under €1,500 ($1,600). The owner spies us and soon sees that we are two newbies. He plays on our insecurities.

"A touring bicycle is a specific thing. It takes you through all kinds of weather, has a sturdy frame, thick tires, strong luggage racks, and is reliable enough to do this day in and day out," he says. "But I wouldn't recommend a basic model for such a long trip."

"What about that bike?" asks Zoë pointing to an old one hanging on the wall.

"That's what people used to cycle around the world in the old days," says the owner. "If you want to repair your bicycle every hundred kilometers, you can," the bike mechanic adds with a chuckle.

We are both thinking the same thing: in the past, the roads were much worse and such lightweight equipment didn't exist. If such bikes survived those conditions, then why on earth wouldn't they now? We go home and start searching the internet for "old road bike," "retro bike," and "vintage bike." Our eyes twinkle when we see the results. We immediately feel the chemistry we missed in the bike shop.

Two days later, we arrive at an apartment building in a suburb. The bikes are standing at the door and look brand new. Two azure Giant Troopers with chrome details, front and rear luggage carriers, 21 gears, down-tube shifters, simple rim brakes, and an old-fashioned dynamo. They are matching women's and men's models.

"These are my parents' bicycles," says Eric, the owner. "Once a year they went cycling for a couple of weeks in Germany and then brought the bikes to the bicycle shop for maintenance. They are at least 25 years old."

"Then they're older than me!" Zoë shouts.

"The old front panniers and handlebar bags are included," says Eric, "I don't believe they are waterproof, but maybe they will come in handy." Ten minutes later we are standing with the bicycles by the trunk of our car having paid only €220 ($235) for both.

"My mom and dad will be happy that their bikes are going around the world. They always dreamed of that. I am glad that you are making that dream come true," Eric tells us.

Turning your dreams into a plan

- Dream out loud, even if it still seems like a vague dream.
- Dare to ask for help. If you don't ask for it, you won't get it.
- Ask, learn, talk, read, and search. The answer comes from being proactive.
- Trust that the answers will come. Suddenly, they will be there.

Our top tips for planning

- Don't plan too far ahead. Life is unpredictable and part of the adventure is discovering as you go.
- Leave enough white space in the planning. The further ahead you plan, the more room there should be for flexibility.
- Don't overestimate yourself physically or mentally. Getting ahead of schedule is much more rewarding than having to catch up.
- It's impossible to do everything. With a goal, you need a schedule and with that comes sacrifice.
- If you have no experience with something, trust your intuition. Take a leap of faith, and test your limits.

Our tips for traveling together

Before you go

- Take time to think and plan together. Brainstorming during an active day in nature can be very inspiring.
- Develop a strong common goal by designing your trip together.
- Discuss individual expectations. Give each other space to think and explain ideas. Don't criticize each other during brainstorming sessions.
- Accept your partner's expectations. Realize that they may differ from yours and support each other.
- Talk about your fears. What do you do if the relationship breaks down on the road? What if someone loses their wanderlust and wants to go home?

On the road

- Your travel companion and life partner is the only person who knows your full story. Other people may have opinions but trust the choices that are best for your relationship. You can only make those together.
- Taking the least painful path is often like running away from the problem. Dare to make the choice that is best in the long run, even if it hurts the most now.

Route planning

Long term

When we set out, we didn't do it with a four-year schedule in mind. We had no idea how long each leg would take or even what some of the legs would consist of. We always wanted to travel in a flexible manner that would allow us to follow our adventure.

Even doing that though, it is useful to have a rough idea of how long a part of the journey might take—whether that is to allow for preparing mentally or knowing the season we will arrive somewhere.

To make a long-term estimate, we calculated an average daily distance which also included rest days.

For example, 62.5 kilometer (39 miles) of cycling per day, plus a rest day every fifth day mean about an average of 50 kilometers (31 miles) a day.

These are examples of the quick-calculating distances we use:

• Cycling: 50 kilometers (31 miles) per day
• Hiking: 20 kilometers (12.5 miles) per day
• Canoeing: 22.5 kilometers (14 miles) per day
• Skiing: 15 kilometers (9.5 miles) per day
• Skating: 30 kilometers (18.5 miles) per day

Day to day, things like terrain, weather, and other factors meant these totals weren't fixed, but everything tended to even out in the end. That meant that we knew that in one month we would cycle about 1,500 kilometers (930 miles) or skate 900 kilometers (560 miles), including rest days.

Short term

Most of the time, we didn't worry too much about short-term planning. We had our route but weren't afraid to deviate from it. We changed courses if we found that a road was too busy, there were no camping spots, or if we received an unexpected invitation.

Every evening we looked at the plan for the next day and adjusted it if necessary. Having a daily goal and mentally preparing for it was important for us. There were, of course, some days when we had to be stricter with our route: for safety reasons in the snow or when we had limited places to resupply.

What tools did we use?

We did almost all of our planning on the computer. While hiking and canoeing, we relied on trail guidebooks.

We usually reviewed the plan for the next day on our phone using a navigation app or Google Maps. Sometimes we just used paper maps, trail guides, or GPS. For the first two years of our trip, we used our phones to navigate. Then we switched to GPS because of its reliability, waterproofing, and better battery life.

How did we plan our route?

We always tried to make use of existing information. The less there was available, the longer the planning process took. We kept to this order:

• Use of established long-distance routes. Such well-established routes usually have GPS files available and sometimes even complete guides with daily distances, sleeping options, and other amenities.
• Google Maps and Google Street View. If there were no existing routes, Google Maps was the starting point for initial planning. We used Google Street View (or satellite photos) to estimate the quality and amount of traffic on a route.
• Open data. Sometimes satellite photos were too old to give reliable travel information. If we needed concrete information, we used open data that was often available on government websites. Road maps showing asphalt and dirt roads were the most useful. We rarely needed to use this step during planning.

Our indispensable travel items

1. **Waka Waka:**
   a solar-powered flashlight and power bank.
2. **Sleeping bag liner:**
   makes the sleeping bag warmer, more hygienic, and more comfortable.
3. **Rain poncho:**
   much more ventilated than a rain suit.
4. **Chopping board:**
   for cutting vegetables, bread, and other food.
5. **Sandals:**
   Zoë's favorite cycling shoes.
6. **An all-purpose knife:**
   for splitting wood, making tent pegs, and so much more.
7. **E-reader:**
   a thousand books packed into 200 grams (7 ounces).
8. **Spotify subscription:**
   for offline music while camping.
9. **Hand saw:**
   indispensable for making campfires.
10. **Seating pad:**
    keeps your butt warm and dry on any surface.

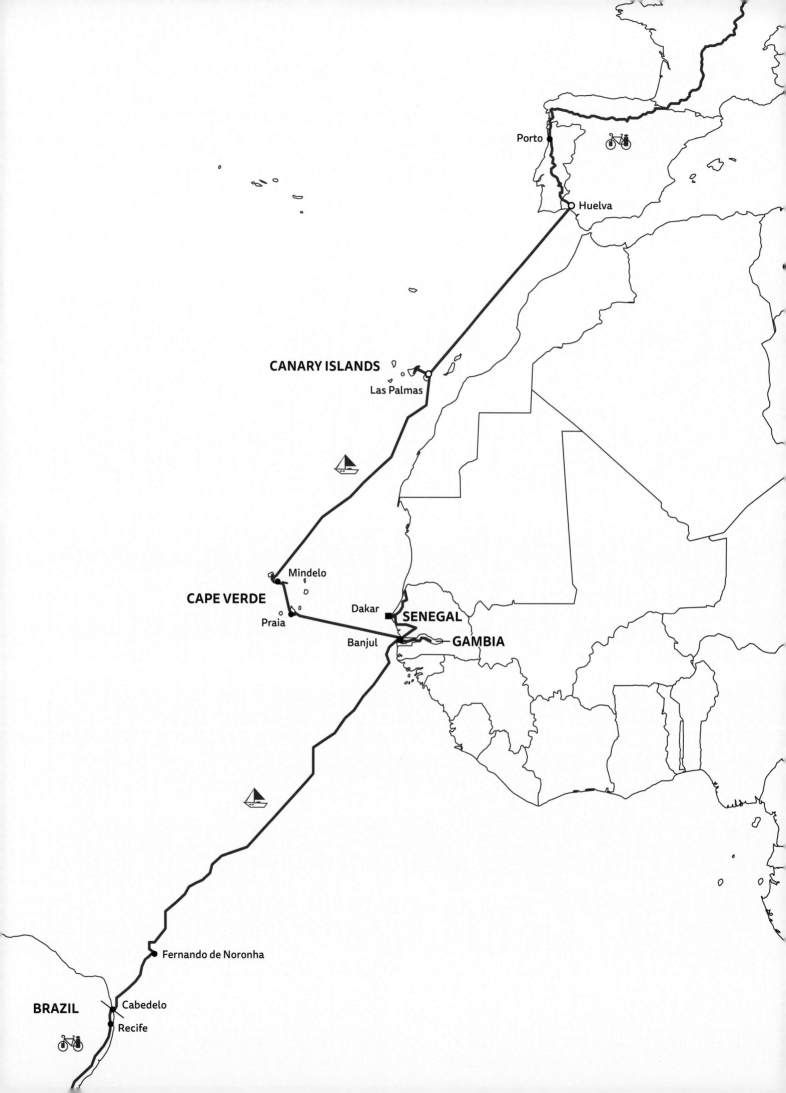

Porto

Huelva

CANARY ISLANDS

Las Palmas

Mindelo

CAPE VERDE

Praia

Dakar

SENEGAL

Banjul

GAMBIA

Fernando de Noronha

BRAZIL

Cabedelo

Recife

THE ATLANTIC CROSSING

Sailing from Gran Canaria to Brazil

We continue our search in Southern Spain but have no luck there. We are told we need to go to the Canaries, which is the hot spot for sailors crossing the ocean. The season starts in December, so we are right on time. We take the ferry from Huelva to Las Palmas in Gran Canaria. Although it's still European, geographically it's much further south and closer to Africa.

We are tense. We aren't even sure whether our dream of sailing is viable, and even if it is, we know nothing about the sailing world and even less about an Atlantic crossing. How do we even go about hitching a lift? How does the search work? We might as well be applying for a job as a cardiac surgeon.

Hitchhiking a Boat

Getting a lift from Gran Canaria

Although winter is about to start, it is 25°C (77°F) and we are walking around the busy harbor in our best t-shirts. There is a wide street with all the sailing stores, cafes, and restaurants on one side. The jetties are on the other side. There are locked steel gates in front of each jetty. If we want to speak to the captains, we will have to get to the other side. "Where do we start?" Zoë asks.

Gradually we distinguish the fellow hitchhikers from the captains and observe their strategies. Some walk around with guitars and play songs, hoping that a lone captain wants to hear some sailor songs on a crossing. Others walk around with cardboard signs of their desired destinations or try their luck at the popular Sailors Bar. It is one of the few places in the harbor with internet service, so all the skippers stop by. We try a more direct approach waiting in front of the jetty gates until someone lets us in. Then we talk to every captain we see.

Our knowledge is honed, and our experience grows day by day. Yet we remain afraid of one thing: what if there is a huge storm, high waves, or waterspouts? Will we capsize or sink in the middle of the ocean? We ask our new friends, John and Raymon, for advice.

"Non-sailors are always afraid of storms," they respond laughing. "The sailboats that cross are seaworthy. Should you find yourself in a big storm, you haul in the sails, go inside, and tightly lock the cabin. The real dangers on a long crossing are seasickness and living together on board."

We breathe a sigh of relief, not knowing that one day those dangers will become reality.

Our main goal is to find a sailboat to cross the Atlantic, but we also explore the Canary Islands by bike. Many professional cyclists and cycling fanatics like us enjoy the challenge of riding to the top of El Teide, the highest mountain in Spain.

Gran Canaria's coastline is densely populated, but the interior is almost deserted. Rugged mountains make it a paradise for hikers and cyclists. Roque Nublo (Rock in the Clouds) is one of Gran Canaria's highest peaks.

Our dream boat

Each day, just before we descend the steps to the harbor, we give ourselves a pep talk. "Today we'll find a boat!" We keep exact records of which boats are new and who we have already spoken to. Soon our little book is full of names, tips, contact details, and new appointments. Our list of requirements is small but important. We want a boat that is outfitted with the necessary safety equipment, and we want to be able to speak the language on board. The captain must be experienced, and we hope there is space to take our bikes.

Sometimes we split up but mostly we work together. We change our greetings and after a while, we no longer say we are hitchhikers. We chat with the captain and find out if there are any opportunities. Every day we are told "no" ten times. We come to accept rejection as normal and walk to the next interview with a smile. Our motivation and energy drop as the days and weeks tick by; it takes mental strength to bounce back from repeated rejection. Every day more and more boats leave without us.

And then, six weeks into our search, out of nowhere, our dream boat arrives. We are watching the Epiphany parade—an important holiday in Spain. In the crowd, Zoë suddenly recognizes a captain.

"Look over there! That's the Swiss couple," Zoë whispers enthusiastically to Olivier.

We had seen them sail into the harbor that afternoon and we immediately walked to where they had docked. However, they looked so exhausted as they disembarked that we intuitively left them alone.

Dieter is 75, and Margrit is almost 70, but she looks a lot younger with her light brown hair. She wears sporty cycling glasses and neat clothes. We ask about hitchhikers and the Atlantic crossing. They tell us that they took a hitchhiker once, but they will never do it again. It was a terrible experience because the boy was seasick, didn't do the dishes well, and barely helped. Our hearts sink, but it is just another "no" to add to the list.

A few days later, Olivier is walking on the jetty and sees Dieter. "What are your food preferences? Can you make up a list of what you eat each day?"

Dieter's question comes out of nowhere. Does that mean what it sounds like? Could it be? We are ecstatic when we realize we might have found a boat. And it is a beautiful boat—a dark blue vessel with two masts and a wooden deck.

We all take a day trip to the other side of the island. On the way back Dieter flatly says, "You can come with us. We are going to Cape Verde, then to Gambia, and finally to Brazil."

We are going sailing.

To make your dream come true
- Hoping for our dream doesn't make it come true. We are responsible for the actions and results ourselves.
- A strong dream is the best motivation. We tell ourselves that it will work and that we are going to do it. We use every muscle until we've succeeded, or we've tried every possible option. We can always adjust our plans, but we don't give up.
- The mind will tell us countless excuses, but there is always a way.

Gran Canaria is an island with many faces. On the north side, surfers enjoy big waves, while in the south the temperature rises to 40 °C (104 °F) in the sand dunes. Every morning we pick oranges, avocados, and bananas from the trees in the garden.

Adopted Parents

Learning the Ropes on the Sailboat to Africa

We are docked at the jetty. Margrit serves us cake on the desk in the cabin. We are made to feel welcome and comfortable, but we have already observed that Margrit and Dieter are quite rigid in their ways. We know that we will have to adapt to that and learn to go with their flow if we are going to get along. We are still aware that we are on their boat. When people invite us into their homes, we adapt our own rhythms and habits to those of the household. It is no different here. Later in the trip, when Zoë's parents visit us in Brazil, her mother says, "It's a wonderful country if you can ride the waves of life." That is what we are starting to do now; we try our best to sail on the Swiss couple's wavelength.

"Always go down like this," demonstrates Dieter as he walks down the steps backward. We imitate him and explore our new home. The kitchen is to the left of the stairs. It has two sinks and a small countertop about half a meter long. There is an oven and four gas burners. Next to the kitchen, there is a dining table surrounded by benches. The boat is actually equipped for six people, so the four of us have plenty of room—relatively speaking. At the front of the boat, there are two doors. Our cabin is on the right and a small toilet is on the left.

In our sleeping berth, two wooden bunk beds are built diagonally above one another. Because the little room is in the bow, the space gets narrower and there isn't enough room for two people to stand. The door has to be closed to open the cupboards, and sitting upright in bed isn't possible. Nonetheless, the small private room is a gift. We are very grateful for all the space we have.

The captain's work area is on the other side of the kitchen. The wall is full of various screens indicating position, speed, depth, and other technical information. The engine room is behind the desk. Dieter explains that the engine was a gift from his sister, given to him when he finally finished constructing his boat after 11 years of manual labor. He proudly tells us that it is one of the best and most expensive engines in the world for this class of boat.

Our plan is to weigh anchor on the weekend, but there is still a lot of work to do. We want to roll up our sleeves and help everywhere, but Dieter doesn't seem so keen on help. Occasionally, Olivier is allowed to assist him, but he never asks Zoë. As the week progresses, "Olivier" is the only thing he says. Dieter takes him out on the water, teaches him to operate the dinghy, and when necessary, Olivier is allowed to go out on his own. He is also allowed to help solve problems on the satellite phone and the AIS system (the advanced GPS that contains all marine traffic). Once in a while, Zoë tries to help proactively by rolling up the lines. Sometimes this is tolerated, but often Dieter tells Olivier to do it. We look at each other when he calls "Olivier" and then shrug. Olivier says "sorry" with his eyes.

Zoë takes on the dishes and cleaning as her regular task—happy to be helping but frustrated at the old-fashioned division of duties. In reality, it hurts her soul. She feels untrusted and redundant. She wants to be so much more than a passenger on this leg of the journey. "Well, it's the way it is. We are guests," she tells herself and Olivier.

On Thursday, it's time to do the grocery shopping. It is a moment we have been looking forward to. This task marks the start of the final countdown. We agree to each pick ten dishes. We put our list of ingredients on the table and add additional supplies for breakfast, lunch, and snacks. The list is huge—20 days of food.

On Saturday morning, during breakfast, Dieter announces, "Today we leave." Dieter and Olivier fill the 600-liter (160-gallon) water tank through a hole in the deck. From now on, we will have to be economical with water. We check that everything is stowed in the cupboards and choose some warm clothes. We have no idea what time we are leaving. We don't dare ask—it doesn't feel right to interrupt Dieter while he is scurrying around completing tasks—so we wait patiently. At 3 p.m., the engine suddenly hums. We quickly position ourselves at the mooring lines and wait for commands. We know we're going by the gas station first to fill up the diesel tank. It's the last stop before we head out on the ocean. Just as when we set off cycling, there is something of the mundane in those first moments of the journey. Even so, we feel full of energy, and our hearts skip as we cruise across the harbor.

"Full!" shouts Zoë, and she jumps back on board after filling the tank. Dieter puts the key in the ignition and turns it. No sound. He removes the key and repeats the action. Again, no sound. Dieter looks pale as he gets up and rechecks all the switches. He tries again. Nothing. We lay low and wait quietly while Dieter crawls through the engine room. "There's water in the engine," says Dieter with a very concerned look. This is the kind of problem that gives a captain an instant migraine. Slowly, the words sink in. There is a good chance that we won't be leaving for a few weeks.

Seasickness

The tension of the past week has been palpable. Every day Dieter has been in the engine compartment trying to find the problem. Each day he identifies a possible source of the problem. We all get our hopes up, only to have them dashed when the engine still fails to start.

Will this attempt be the right one? Dieter's face gives us confidence that he's finally fixed the issue. It is a little before 2 p.m. when the engine hums again. The atmosphere instantly relaxes, and we dare to allow our excitement to build. Dieter orders us to cast off the ropes while he calmly maneuvers the boat out of the dock. Our port neighbors realize that we are leaving. With loud honks of their horns, they wave goodbye. This place has been our home for a month and a half. We know almost all the boats from piers A to T. We've walked past the same stores and bars so

In the harbor of Las Palmas, there are over 1,000 sailing boats. In November, the Atlantic Rally for Cruisers (ARC) attracts over 200 sailing boats to participate (previous page). On the ocean, there is nothing around us but water. Life becomes simple.

many times. Everything is familiar from the smell of the harbor and the clattering of the masts to the creaking of the jetty and the clicking of the jetty gates. But now we are finally venturing into the unknown. We sail out on the ocean feeling like heroes. We are off, on our way to Africa!

Soon we have left Las Palmas behind and are sailing further and further out into the ocean. We listen to Dieter's instructions, and Olivier is allowed to help hoist the sails, although he only holds on to the line while Dieter energetically turns the winch. The sails have been set, the wind is now coming from behind, and the boat begins its rhythmic sway on the waves. We follow the trade wind, which roars from Europe to the west coast of Africa and South America.

We sail day and night. The night watches are the main reason sailors bring a "crew." The first evening is not a real night watch, but we keep Dieter company in the cockpit. He doesn't want us to be on watch alone yet, and we understand that. We have no experience, and there is quite a bit of traffic around the island. Moreover, we have no idea what to do if a ship suddenly appears in front of us, the wind picks up, or the autopilot goes crazy. We carefully watch what Dieter does and learn what to look out for. Every ten minutes, we scan the ocean to see if there are lights on the horizon. Every now and then, Dieter adjusts the sails or changes course by a few degrees on the GPS. Keeping him company is not a difficult task. Dieter quickly says that he enjoys the quiet that nighttime brings to the ocean. He has no desire to talk, so for hours, we stare quietly at the inky rolling waves. Olivier reads a book on his e-reader but is soon hanging overboard emptying the contents of his stomach. On Dieter's advice, he gets into bed and does feel better after some rest.

On the vast ocean, we are like a small bar of soap being carried from one wave to the next. The horizon is empty on all sides with only the sun providing any sense of direction and time. We quickly learn to adjust our pace of life—sometimes the days feel as empty as the ocean. The possibility of seeing another ship—perhaps 15 miles away—is a moment of excitement, but more often than not, the only sign of others is a triangular symbol on the GPS.

In the morning, everyone gets up when they want. Dieter and Margrit alternate watches and ask us to pay attention for three minutes when they boil hot water for tea. For Olivier—still nauseous—breakfast consists of dry muesli which takes him almost an hour to eat. Most of the time we sit at the front of the boat or on the edge of the cockpit. We enjoy the slow movement and the solitude of the vast ocean. We often see dolphins swimming next to the boat, jumping in front of the bow, or even somersaulting over the waves. In the excitement, Olivier's seasickness disappears but only for a short while.

After three days, Olivier develops sunken cheeks and a dull expression in his eyes. The seasickness doesn't go away. Eating and drinking become a major effort, and Zoë forces him to empty his plate every time. "Not that much!" he protests as she scoops extra granola into his bowl. No matter how delicious all the meals look, Olivier never has an appetite. The ocean gets wilder, with waves up to 5 meters (16 feet) in quick succession.

There are no more naps on the deck, and the waves are too wild for whale watching. One night, we are truly scared for the first time. The waves pound against the ship and the mast creaks from top to bottom. Each wave creates a blow like a hammer. We imagine the mast snapping and the water rushing in on us. The immense power of the ocean makes us feel small and fragile, and we wonder how the boat can withstand so much power. But the boat sails on, day and night. Just like our captain. The indestructible Dieter navigates us through the turbulent seas with long hours on deck.

Olivier often sits against the mast toward the bow. That is the place where the boat moves the least. His eyes are empty, and he is thin and lifeless. The seasickness is slowly breaking him mentally and physically. He can't think rationally, and he starts to question what he is doing on the trip. It is a grueling experience. Unlike car sickness, there is no stopping for fresh air. A sailboat can feel like a prison when you're seasick and the nausea saps your ability to do even the most basic of tasks. Olivier tries scanning the horizon for land but finds none. He now fully understands the well-known saying: "You are truly seasick when you no longer fear death but fear that you will continue living."

The strong wind blows us to Africa. After six days and nights, land is in sight. We drop anchor and spend the night floating just off the coast to avoid the risks of docking in the dark. The next morning, we sail into the port of Mindelo in Cape Verde with a feeling of pride. Olivier begins to emerge from the dark embrace of his seasickness, and we focus on what we have achieved. We've made it to Africa on a sailboat!

A container vessel is moored in the harbor of Mindelo, Cape Verde. Olivier lies still to alleviate his seasickness (opposite). The horizon is flat in all directions, making the sunsets spectacular, undisturbed, and exuberant. When the sun rises again 12 hours later, the ocean looks unchanged (above).

Persistence

Sailing from Cape Verde to Gambia

Ask a sailor why they love sailing and the answer is often, "It is the highest form of freedom. We are detached from the world, follow our own path, and are completely self-sufficient and independent." After seven days of seasickness, Olivier has begun to think otherwise. Joyfully, he jumps into the water of Mindelo harbor and enjoys the warm African sun. We are more than 1,000 kilometers (620 miles) closer to the equator. Luxury sailing yachts are scattered among rusty sunken shipwrecks that protrude from the water. An old cruise ship is half beached on the land, and poor fishermen putter by in small wooden motorboats. It's a strange contrast between luxury and poverty.

Dieter and Margrit are tired after the long trip. After seven nights at sea, we cook a luxurious breakfast of bacon, eggs, and baked beans. We want to get ashore as soon as possible, but it's Sunday and all immigration services are closed. We are both yearning to get away from the boat, hit dry land, and stretch our legs. Carefully we convince Dieter and Margrit. "This is Africa. There is no one waiting to check our passport," we urge.

We need a few days to recover from our first voyage. Mentally, we are not ready for the next part. Olivier in particular has completely lost his desire to travel. He's lost 5 kilos (11 pounds), and his stomach still hasn't recovered. We can't shake a sense of foreboding when we think about our future plans. We will be living together with Margrit and Dieter for three months, island-hopping our way toward South America. On the other hand, we are extremely grateful to Dieter and Margrit for the opportunity.

After a week on shore, we leave for the next island. At first, we sail smoothly among small waves. Olivier sits on the deck, smiling. "Today I'm not seasick!" he says confidently to Zoë. After two hours, we reach the southern tip of the island and turn west. The peaceful swaying immediately changes to a wild ocean. The sails start flapping, and the waves crash against the boat. The boat is headed into the wind, and we have to deviate from our course, then power directly into the wind using the engine. Olivier's face turns white and soon his breakfast disappears into the sea. He lies on his bed with a bucket next to his head. After 12 hours of sailing, we are still far from our destination, so the torture continues endlessly. Olivier's stomach contents disappear into a bucket over 10 times. He refuses to eat or drink, and his vomit has turned a dark green. Olivier is a miserable sight as he slumps on the bed.

Cape Verde is an archipelago consisting of ten volcanic islands, some with beach resorts, others with steep mountains. Santo Antão is a hiking paradise and offers us an escape from the sailboat.

Cape Verde is also called "Africa for Beginners." Beautiful houses and paved roads alternate with stone huts, cobblestone roads, and simple roadside stalls which serve as clothing stores and restaurants.

Our original plan was to visit as many islands as possible in Cape Verde. Strong winds and difficult sailing decide otherwise. We sail from São Vicente and São Nicolau to Santiago where we prepare for the crossing to Gambia in mainland Africa. For us, Santo Antão is the most beautiful island.

We arrive well after midnight, and the visibility is almost zero. We need to anchor down, and this requires all hands on deck. Olivier sits on his knees, bent over the anchor, and repeatedly gives all his strength to raise and drop the anchor. Each time it doesn't hold, and we are blown into the ocean by the strong wind. At 4 a.m., we are finally anchored. Olivier is bone tired.

"Zoë, I don't want anymore," he whispers, and his eyes fall shut. After two months of seasickness, Olivier has had all he can take. A few days before we arrive in Gambia, he lays his cards on the table. He has made up his mind that his sailing journey is over when we reach our next layover. With our longest sailing stretch still to come, his decision is both pragmatic and borne out of desperation. "I won't survive 20 days without eating and drinking." And with that, our journey faces a crossroads.

Tips for first-time adventurous travel

- Do something unfamiliar, new, or exciting every day. This increases your confidence to embrace the unknown and trust your instincts.
- Start with small goals. When we set off, even the south of Spain seemed very far to us. If we had set the goal of 40,000 kilometers (25,000 miles), we would have never started. Hourly, daily, and weekly objectives keep you moving without being overwhelmed.
- Give yourself four weeks to adjust. After that, anything new will become part of your routine, and then you can make an honest judgment. You may learn that something isn't for you, but you will do so knowing that you have given it your all.

The main language of Cape Verde is Portuguese, and Creole, a mixture between Portuguese and African languages, is also widely spoken.
A mother and her son try to explain the rules of Mancala to us, but the language barrier makes it difficult for us to understand each other.

Different Paths

Olivier's Solo Trip to Senegal

For two weeks, Zoë has been lying awake with mixed feelings. Olivier has made up his mind, but what should she do? Continue or leave the boat too? To get off means to give up and those words aren't in her dictionary. Continuing means leaving Olivier behind and is that what she really wants? She can't make up her mind. One moment she's sure she shouldn't let this opportunity pass her by. The next moment her stomach fills with doubt once again.

We lie on the bed in our cabin and look at the starry sky through the open window above our heads. "What are you going to do while I am sailing?" Zoë asks.

"I don't know. The cheapest way to Brazil is to fly from Dakar. So, I'll travel in Senegal for a while, I guess," but he doesn't sound very convincing. We'd rather not fly but it's the only option for Olivier. "And you? Have you decided?"

"I don't know what I want anymore," Zoë says with tears in her eyes. We stare out the window until Olivier says, "You have to do it! Three weeks of suffering and be proud the rest of your life or give up and always have lingering regrets. Don't think about me. I want you to make your dream come true." Zoë turns and curls up with Olivier. "I don't want to miss you."

We resolve to take different paths. We know it will be painful for now, but certainly, it will be worth it. We get some negative feedback from friends and family. Zoë in particular has a hard time because many people think it is selfish of her to leave seasick Olivier behind. We are steadfast. It is *our* journey. Outsiders, no matter how close, only know part of the story. It is one of the hardest decisions we have had to make together but perhaps the best. It is a testament to unconditional love. We already miss each other and look forward to the moment Zoë arrives in Brazil.

Cape Verde was a warm-up; this is the real Africa. Life in Gambia is exuberant, colorful, and immensely rich in culture. We explore the beaches and the inland using the same transportation as the locals. The fuller the better seems to be the only rule of thumb.

On Dieter's calendar next to his worktable, there is a circle around April 3rd, the departure date for the Atlantic crossing. The days before are marked with a thick line representing preparation. "You cannot be on the boat the last three days," says Dieter. "We have to prepare mentally with the crew." Olivier is disappointed, but he accepts what Dieter says. He won't be able to see the boat leave. He is no longer part of it.

The last meal – *Olivier*

The atmosphere has been strange these past few days. I want to spend every minute together with Zoë, knowing that we won't see each other for a month. But there isn't much room for romance. Yesterday was my birthday; the day before, I had to get off the boat. It could have been a farewell party after two months of sailing, but I didn't have that feeling. I felt mostly sad. The boat was my house for two months but never my home. There were beautiful moments where we felt invincible on the big ocean, moments of laughter with Dieter and Margrit, but also days of seasickness filled with frustration. From setbacks, we learn the most, and yes, I have learned a lot these past two months. It's an experience I'll never forget but will never do again.

Today is the day. I get off the boat and head to Senegal, but Dieter needs my help one last time. My last ride is 500 meters (1,650 feet) to the water and diesel station. Dieter and I raise the anchor. It's a task that Zoë is still not allowed to do, just like everything else that requires "masculine" strength. Who knows, maybe she'll be allowed to help when I'm gone. We fill the boat with water and 400 liters (106 gallons) of diesel.

"You can go if you want," Dieter says. Goodbye foster parents, goodbye boat. A feeling of emptiness overtakes me. When I was seasick, all I wanted was to get off the boat. Now it feels like giving up, like failing. I keep telling myself that I made the right choice. Deep down I know it's true, but it doesn't make leaving any easier.

A giant baobab tree serves as a billboard in the center of a small town (opposite). Fishermen nap under a *pirogue*, a handmade wooden boat, on a beach in Tanji (above).

The crossing – *Zoë*

We walk hand in hand to the ferry. We hold each other tightly. Olivier carries his backpack. I squeeze his hand and a heavy feeling fills my throat. I already miss him. What a way to say goodbye. This feeling is unusual, unfamiliar, and indescribable. We have both thought about this for a long time and we have made a deliberate decision together. Instinctively, I compartmentalize my emotions and try to prepare for the journey that lies ahead.

Olivier buys a ticket for the ferry and has to follow the crowd. We give each other a last kiss through the closed gate. "I love you," "I already miss you," "I love you too," and there isn't time for anything else. Olivier disappears in the crowd. I stand still for a moment to process the emotions. "Goodbye my love, I'm going to miss you." I take a deep breath, make myself strong, turn around, and start off on my own adventure.

Now it's Margrit, Dieter, and me. M&D, as I write in my diary. We are different people, we have different ideas, and are different ages. We like each other and respect each other, but actually, we have very little in common. We don't want to get in each other's way, but we often do. Why do I want this so badly? I cycled 4,000 kilometers (2,485 miles) with the idea of crossing the ocean. Now I have come this far, and I have to finish it. But for whom?

I am doing this for myself. I want to overcome myself. This expedition is not in "the easiest boat," but it is the right challenge. It is a learning experience, I think as I walk back to the boat. Yesterday Olivier said the words he knew I needed to hear. "It's a unique challenge. It's a life experience, where you have to learn to adapt to the situation, and there is no escape."

When I get back on the boat, I immediately feel alone. They don't ask a word about the goodbye, not a word is said about Olivier. Life goes on as if no one had left. No question, no smile. Am I ready for this?

A woman sells vegetables from her own garden at the market in Bakau (opposite). A group of women wait for a ferry that crosses the Gambia River in Lamin Koto, deep in inner Gambia. They are wearing colorful dresses for a wedding ceremony (above).

Women work in a salt mine in Saint-Louis, in northern Senegal. They barely earn €0.25 ($0.27) for 25 kilos (55 pounds) of salt. Women in Sokone with more sustainable and healthier woodstoves for cooking (opposite, top & bottom right).

The Doldrums Ahead

Feeling Lonely on the Atlantic

Dieter busies himself making plans for the coming trip. There is no discussion, and it makes me feel nervous and left out. I remind myself that these days of preparation will be the hardest. Once we sail, I can focus on myself. We buy 20 kilos (44 pounds) of potatoes, 10 kilos (22 pounds) of onions, and 90 eggs. We walk through the dark but colorful markets of Banjul. It's a long route over the same sandy roads, past the same store, past the same people who make us pay too much time and time again, past the same children who recognize us and ask for candies again, into the same dinghy that we have to inflate every trip and to the same sailboat, in which we will soon cross the ocean. I walk behind Dieter and Margrit, or sometimes in front of them. The tears roll down my cheeks. It is time to go.

According to the navigation system, the crossing will be 2,000 nautical miles, which is equal to 3,700 kilometers (2,300 miles). Dieter calculates a duration of 16 to 18 days at most. I play it safe and prepare myself for a 20-day trip. That would be possible even if the boat was moving much slower than normal.

When I look at the weather maps, it looks windless, especially the doldrums—the wind still area around the equator. By now, I know that Dieter hardly ever looks at weather maps. I ask some sailing friends from Las Palmas for help and get varying feedback. One says it's nice and calm, and I should enjoy it. The other says we should definitely not leave. Of course, it's only the negative words that stick. I sit in my cabin and bury my face in my hands. I know that I should leave it up to the captain.

On the day before departure, I can't hold it anymore. "Dieter, I've been looking at different weather charts; they predict very low winds," I tell him. "Hmm," is all he says.

Even more fools

Totally unexpectedly, a German boat sails out of the Gambia River and anchors 100 meters (330 feet) from our boat. I jump into the water and swim over. They say the crocodiles are only further out in the mangroves; I hope so. My need for companionship is so great. As it turns out, the other boat is also leaving this afternoon! And yes, also to Brazil. A sense of security overwhelms me. We won't be alone, and we won't be the only ones crossing this late in the season. What reassurance!

"The weather doesn't look good, does it?" says Claus. I'm glad I can talk to another sailor about the weather. That is, until he boasts, "But I'm not worried. I have a 1,000-liter tank and 200 liters stored on deck just to be on the safe side." My heart skips a beat. We have about 400 liters (106 gallons) and a 20-liter (5.3-gallon) jerry can on deck. I swim back to our boat. We are both leaving at the end of the afternoon. At high tide, when the water flows out of the river, I notice that Margrit and Dieter find peace in the Germans' company too. For me, Claus and Ingrid are a gift. I am so glad that we will have another sailboat by our side. At 3 p.m., Dieter is behind. He is working on his blog, but he still has to check the electronic equipment. It all feels so unprepared. At 4 p.m., we see Claus sail by. "Have a good trip!" they shout. No! Stop, wait for us, I think.

I am plagued by anxiety and mixed emotions. I try to reach Olivier one last time before we sail out. I can't get hold of him. Damn Olivier! It's almost 6 p.m., and I'm starting to think that we may leave tomorrow when Dieter says, "Okay, we're pulling the anchor in." I take a deep breath and put myself at the anchor. For the first time in two months, I share the hauling with Dieter and he accepts my help! The boat turns with a powerful swing toward the Atlantic. I stand with my face in the wind and feel the excitement. We are leaving! The big trip!

As we set sail, I let Olivier's phone ring 100 times, but he doesn't answer. I send a last message and hope he still responds.

3/4/2017 19:09] Zoë: Darling!

3/4/2017 19:09] Zoë: Pick up!

3/4/2017 19:10] Zoë: I want to tell you that I love you! And can't wait to see you! Can grab hold of you! Can kiss and lay on your chest! You can imagine me every night, curling up next to you and giving you a very warm, long kiss!

Olivier finally calls me back. I answer hastily. I don't know what to say anymore; I can't find the right words. When I hang up, I collect my thoughts. All I know is that I am extremely fond of him. I am so happy with this man, who not only respects my choices but also encourages them.

Then the bars on my iPhone are empty and it says "no connection." Those are the last words from my phone for the next 20 days. In this world, we can hardly isolate ourselves without seeing people or man-made objects around us and getting distracted. It's difficult to connect with anything. I realize that this is the strange, special, and unique thing about this trip. This is the experience I want.

A forced relationship

I create a schedule to hold on to during the structureless days ahead. It's an agenda that doubles as a table to record statistics. Every day at 6 p.m., I write down our position in GPS coordinates, the distance traveled, our average speed, the water consumption, how much diesel we used, and how many engine hours we burn.

I think it would be smart if I did night watches. Dieter hadn't allowed us to do that so far. I can't resist discussing the subject. Night watches are an exhausting task to do alone for 20 days. I sit quietly with the captain and wait for a good moment.

"It's going to be a long trip. It's important that everyone stays fit," I say. "Why don't I keep watch some nights? You can sleep in the cockpit, and I promise I'll wake you up the moment anything happens." Surprisingly, Dieter accepts, and it feels like a victory. I will be on watch every day from 4 a.m. to 8 a.m.

There is no wind for the first 24 hours. Last night we hardly moved at all. We start our "sailing" trip with 12 engine hours and finish the first day with an average of 2.8 knots per hour. At this rate, it will take us about a month to make the trip. On the second day, we are at least able to make progress using the wind. We are not going fast but at least no zero appears on the speedometer.

The sea is calm. It moves like a big magic carpet, with light, slowly billowing waves. Olivier could have handled this. We just calmly sway back and forth. Cooking can be done without the risk of being burned by boiling water and getting seasick seems almost impossible. I must admit, although it is slow, it sure is comfortable.

The first week feels more like just a couple of days on the undulating ocean. The gentle wind doesn't come from the right direction, so we zigzag our way along, tacking toward the southwest. That means changing sails at least six times a day. We can't complain; we are still making progress and are back on my 20-day schedule.

Meanwhile, I work on building a bond with Margrit. She is a serious woman and quite different from my mother who raised me to be independent. I let her braid my hair and ask her a lot about her daughter. I tell her everything that comes to mind. It works, Margrit and I grow closer. I'm not entirely myself, but I slowly gain her respect. I get to see the caring woman under the stern exterior—uncertain, tender, and kind.

Despite our budding relationship—or perhaps because of it—the first week is pretty hard. It takes energy to play a role that isn't really me. In addition, I have been accepted as a "seafaring woman," which is great. But now I also feel the physical exhaustion

An old sailing ship is anchored next to us in the harbor of Mindelo. This harbor is a popular stop and resupply spot for sailboats crossing the Atlantic Ocean.

On the first leg from Gran Canaria to Cape Verde, the ocean was turbulent with continuous 5-meter (16-foot) waves. From Gambia to Brazil, the ocean is often completely flat (this page). Flying fish often end up on top of the deck when they try to escape predators (opposite).

of sailing. We don't have much or sometimes no electricity. The wind turbine doesn't turn when the winds are low, and the sails block the solar panels. That means we have to switch off the autopilot. We have to steer ourselves, and Dieter can't do that alone. We sail 24/7 manually using only a compass. It's fun for the first few days, but it's tough work. Day in, and day out, we alternated the helmsman every two hours. Add in the night watches and cooking duties, and we all get quickly exhausted. We do little other than sleep in between our sailing shifts.

Week 2

In the second week, I let go. Dieter and Margrit are set in their ways, and while they entertain my suggestions, their decisions always stay the same. In the end, it is easier just to accept the status quo. I try to be useful by preparing a nice meal every afternoon and by cleaning the boat. In the moments when I sit in the shadow of the sails, I enjoy some of the wonders of the ocean. The sun's rays disappear into infinite depths under the blue surface. They make me see further than I really can. They make me realize that there are 3,000 meters (9,800 feet) of water under me and I begin to imagine what is going on there. Seabirds live in the middle of the ocean and regularly roam around our boat. We move through the water like a whale and flying fish spread their wings in an attempt to flee from us. Magic abounds in the evening. The sunsets are full of color and exuberance. The sky is sparkling and nowhere is it brighter than around the equator. Beside the boat, twinkling lights illuminate the jet-black water. I wonder what they are—so powerful, so bright. I'm not surprised that early sailors thought they were being visited by mythical female creatures. The reality is as spectacular as the myth. Bioluminescent algae light up in this dazzling way when disturbed. Sometimes it's so bright, I think a flashlight is shining on me. It is truly magical!

On day 14, at the end of the second week, we sail straight toward a beautiful rainbow. Like a finish line arch, it points the way to the equator. Precisely under our multicolored banner, the geographic coordinates change to 00.0000 degrees. We cross into the southern half of the globe. Other than the ephemeral rainbow, there is no sign to mark our crossing. The ocean is the same blue and the same size. Everything is the same, yet we think it is time for celebration and Margrit bakes a cake. The ocean is so calm that we can enjoy our cake at the table with a knife, fork, and glass of apple juice.

Dieter doesn't know the exact size of his diesel tank, so we have no idea how much diesel we actually have. We are just over halfway, but the tank seems almost empty. We have had to use the engine so many times through windless areas. It's driving me crazy. The fear of running out of petrol consumes me and fills me with dread.

I spend a lot of time in my cabin. Because the ocean is so calm, I can lie in bed without difficulty. For hours at a stretch, I just read. Dieter tells me I'm not allowed to do the night watches anymore. I don't know why, but I don't mind. I fill my day with little tasks. Every night in bed, I miss Olivier intensely. I imagine him next to me and fantasize about having sex with him. I want his soft hand, his kisses, and his warm body. I feel lonely, but my fantasies help. He feels very close at those moments. Sometimes I cry and write about how much I miss him in my diary. Then I fight

against loneliness. It won't last. I am energized by the isolation. I know I can handle difficult situations, and I feel enriched by my experiences and the lessons I've learned.

I mark the end of the day by taking a shower. It is a moment of privacy and seclusion that I look forward to every evening. After saying, "I'm taking a shower," I stand in front of the sails, stark naked at the tip of the bow, and loosen my hair. It flutters in the wind as I pour buckets of salt water over me and let the sun warm me. I sit on my knees and feel the gentle breeze slide over my wet skin. I feel free, open, and alive. I close my eyes and breathe the fresh air through my nose. There I sit, and yet no one sees me. I look at the water, the immense distance, and listen to the serene silence around me.

Week 3

All day extremely dark rain clouds from the west, north, and east are closing in on our boat. Last night, the gods warned us with lightning bolts signaling that they were approaching. We are sailing right into the open gap, toward the blue sky. The angry sky looks beautiful. The ocean is more turbulent than usual, and despite the light breeze, she shows that she has energy to burn. I see the dark ocean change in an ominous way. Vortexes appear, rolling their way down from the low-hanging clouds. Oh no! Waterspouts! I'm in the middle of the Atlantic with an almost empty diesel tank and three tornadoes right in front of me. This cannot be true. I can't quite estimate how far away they are. A wild guess tells me 10 kilometers (33 feet), but these raging twisters move ultrafast. Soon we'll be in the middle of them. Surely, we'll lose a mast. Then what? Fear ripples through my body as I call out to Dieter.

"That's the last thing we need," he mutters as he looks open-mouthed and wide-eyed at the tornadoes. We keep a tight eye on them as we race towards the blue window of safety. The southwest wind pushes them back, and after two hours, they are gone. The goosebumps on my skin take a little longer to disappear.

Love in Paradise

Together Again in Fernando de Noronha

We need diesel. The tank is almost empty, and if the wind stays like this, we will have a problem. We are incredibly lucky that there is an island 400 kilometers (250 miles) off the Brazilian coast called Fernando de Noronha. From there, it's another three to five days to the mainland. I can't believe my ears. Dieter suddenly suggests we stay a week and let Olivier come to the island. What a kind gesture. I feel intense happiness.

I lie down with my belly on the deck and am welcomed by a group of dolphins. They dance and jump around the boat. They know it too. I'm about to see Olivier! They come to celebrate with me. I reach out toward the water. I can almost touch them, and it feels as if I can talk to them. They give me the companionship I have been longing for. I feel joy, victory, and pride. I close my eyes and promise myself to remember this moment forever. When I open them again, I see a powerful spray in the distance water. An unwieldy mass rises to the surface. I squeeze my eyes closed to slits. There she is, the largest animal on earth—the whale!

After 19 days on the water, I see a few gray outlines on the horizon. "Land in sight!" I shout to Dieter and Margrit who take the binoculars and want to see themselves. This is how the first explorers must have felt. Although it is not the final stop, it feels like an enormous victory. Tears of happiness fill my eyes. Then, without warning, the engine stops.

"No, this can't be true," sighs Dieter. The last stretch is against the wind, and without the engine, we'll drift past the islands. Dieter checks the engine, but everything seems normal. The cheerful atmosphere of 10 minutes ago has disappeared. Dieter puts a long stick into the intake and feels a large lump. "There is something stuck in the water inlet," I hear him say to Margrit. Suddenly he shouts, "We are having fish for dinner." For two weeks now, the fishing line has been hanging out at the back of the boat to no avail. We breathe a sigh of relief. The poor fish is dead, but the engine is healthy again.

Slowly, far too slowly, we get closer. I am hungry with impatience when we finally anchor down and get into the dinghy to sail to land. As soon as we land, I forget to kiss the sand. There is just one thing on my mind: Olivier! I say goodbye to Dieter and Margrit and hurry to the small airport.

As I enter the lobby and peer through the glass. I am just in time; the plane has just landed. Then I see Olivier waiting in line. He doesn't see me. It's a surprise, though I think he expects it. Suddenly he looks straight in my direction. I quickly pull my head away, but when I peek again, he has a big smile on his face.

This is Praia do Sancho, often selected as the most beautiful beach in Brazil. 70 percent of Fernando de Noronha is a protected nature reserve. Only 500 tourists are permitted on the island at a time, making almost every beach a private one.

The life above and below sea is the main attraction on Fernando de Noronha. There are a few endemic species, like the Noronha skink, one of the two endemic reptiles found on the island (opposite).

We both feel giddy when our eyes meet. There's so much to tell, so many emotions, and so much love to catch up on. The timing is perfect. We have three full days together on the most beautiful island in the world—the best gift we could have ever asked for.

We listen, cuddle, talk, cuddle, walk, and cuddle some more. Every question is answered, every story told. We look at each other and grab each other's hands. Tears come regularly. We feel closer to each other than ever before. We are unconditionally in love. We walk along the coastline. Olivier had African pants made for Zoë in Senegal. We are almost the same size, so he bought some fabric from a lady and asked a tailor to make a pair of pants exactly the way Zoë likes them. Olivier watches the loose pants flutter around Zoë's slender body. She feels Olivier's eyes which makes her feel beautiful.

When night falls, and we are sure we are alone, we finally make love. It goes very quietly, very tenderly. We look at each other. The tips of our fingers slowly touch each other. Our hearts race. We feel everything intensely. The three days fly by, but they are and will always be the most romantic days of our lives.

After our three days together, we return to reality. Zoë to the sailboat and Olivier to the mainland. For Zoë, there will be three days of sailing to the marina in Cabedelo. After spending time with Olivier, somehow those last three days feel even longer than the previous three weeks of sailing.

What we have learned about our relationship
- Love is so much stronger when there is respect, space, and encouragement for each other's individual desires in addition to common goals.
- We all have tough moments. They are a time for compassion, a smile, a hug, and some motivation. That's how we build each other up.
- We seem destined for each other, but that is because we overcome everything that drives us apart. We need each other, make each other stronger, and cannot live without each other.

Everything Is Different Alone

How Olivier Travels to Brazil

After Zoë drops me off at the ferry, I keep looking back until I can no longer see her. The passengers are packed together like sardines, and the ferry slowly sails across the wide mouth of the Gambia River in the blazing sun. I catch myself looking around for Zoë. It has become an instinctive reaction, but I am alone. Zoë is not here. We have been in each other's company for so long—always exchanging glances, words, and smiles. Now I am alone, crammed between hundreds of people.

A little later, I am on an old bus headed to Toubacouta. A 20-year-old woman sits down next to me.

"Are you alone here?" she asks immediately. "I have a house in Sokone. Do you come with me?"

She clearly doesn't mince words. I try to explain that I have a girlfriend who is on a sailboat in Gambia, but my effort to deter her has the opposite effect.

"You need a girl here too," she continues, swaddling her baby on her lap.

When I get off the bus, I quickly look for my own place to sleep. It feels strange to walk around alone and not be able to ask Zoë, "What do you think about this?" We are used to making decisions as a couple, but now I have to

ask myself what I want. One advantage of traveling alone is that you learn to make your own decisions. For a moment, I feel liberated, but once I plop down on the bed, I stare at the ceiling, lonely.

160 characters

As the days go by, I thankfully worry a little less about Zoë. Twice a day I look at the map and, after five days, I can still see the boat in my mind. After the slow start, they seem to be making good progress, which makes me optimistic about their successful arrival in Brazil. After five days, it's time to send a message to the satellite phone—our only means of staying in touch. I can send as many messages as I want, but I know too many would drive Dieter crazy. Once every five days seems fair, along with the occasional weather update.

The message can contain up to 160 characters. I develop an improvised and almost secret language when I send a message, trying to summarize five days of emotions and experiences into the length of a text message. Then I have to wait for a reply that arrives in my email. The rest I have to fill in with my own imagination.

A glimmer of hope

The beaches in Senegal are known as the most beautiful in Africa, but they don't appeal to me. If I have learned one thing in the past two weeks, it is that I am not as good at being alone as I thought. I am a soloist who prefers to choose his own path and likes to be independent. But after two weeks in Senegal, I am anything but entertained. I am just waiting out the time.

Three days later, I'm on a plane to Brazil. Zoë is only halfway there, so I'll arrive way before her. When I see the ocean from the air, it doesn't seem so mighty at all. I see a vague dark blue mass, but I can't get a sense of proportion. I throw an imaginary rope from the plane and pull the sailboat across a little faster. I arrive in Recife and see that I have a message from the satellite phone.

"LongbfISeeY.owind.standstill.fewdiesel. mk Stpvr/3d Islnd F.n. SeeLonelyp.daycost high.guess16dtomainland:(.goodflight.mom: locationcorrct.kiss"

Sixteen more days. That feels endless. My glimmer of hope is "Islnd F.n." I have no idea what it means, but the word "island" gives me some reassurance.

Diego changes his ways

At 1 a.m., I ring Diego's doorbell. A man covered in tattoos with a long beard and wild hair opens the steel prison-like door. A big smile appears on his face. *"Bem-vindo à minha casa,"* he says as he swings open the heavy door. Diego comes from the southernmost province of Brazil, Rio Grande do Sul, more than 3,000 kilometers (1,850 miles) from Recife. He studied computer science there, and he started his own company. His entrepreneurial spirit and social character are a great advantage in the computer world. Soon he earned a lot of money and found himself on the wrong track. With long working days, a lot of stress, and constant pressure at work, he became addicted to cocaine. At his lowest point, he wasted a fortune on drugs every week. He was on the brink of death.

"If I had continued for one more week, I would have died of an overdose or been killed by a drug cartel," Diego tells me.

After a month in a closed institution, he spent five months in rehabilitation on a farm. Slowly he crawled out of the pit and gained new life energy, and—even more importantly—a new perspective on life. Money was no longer important to him; it had been replaced by a desire to do what he loved and be happy every day. He has dreamed of doing a world bike trip to symbolize his regained freedom and independence. Three days ago, I sent him a message through Warmshowers. He is overjoyed with my arrival, and I am happy to have some company.

I originally never wanted to go to Brazil because of all the fear-driven TV coverage. Robberies, drugs, cartels, favelas—you name it. The media portrays a life-threatening country. After a few days in Recife, I still have all my belongings and walk through the streets carefree. Brazil is not dangerous, nor is Gambia, Senegal, or all the other countries we visit later. Of course, there is poverty and violence, but that's not exclusive to foreign lands.

Then Diego reminds me not to become too complacent. "He jumped on the road and pointed his gun at me." Diego reenacts the incident from half an hour ago. On his way home, he was almost mugged by an armed man. "Nothing happened," he laughs, "I raised my middle finger and quickly cycled on."

Into my arms

The lady behind the counter at the airport on Fernando de Noronha must be wondering why I am so happy to pay the expensive tourist tax to visit the island.

All the longing of the past weeks turns into joy. Never before have I felt so much in love. We fall into each other's arms and don't let go until a luggage cart pushes against my leg and wants to pass.

I take Zoë to a small restaurant where she can finally eat something different than potatoes, onions, and eggs. She looks skinny and emotionally wrung out.

"What happened to you?" I wonder aloud. Zoë bursts into tears but can't explain.

"Nothing, nothing—it was actually really good. We had a nice trip," she says through all the tears.

All of her suppressed emotions from the past three weeks come out. I listen to her stories with admiration and indignation. What an out-of-this-world adventure. Not for a second do I feel jealous, only proud. Only Zoë could have done all this.

BRAZIL

Fernando de
Noronha

Cabedelo
Recife

Aracaju

Salvador

Brasilia

São Paulo

CHILE

Porto Alegre

ARGENTINA

Mendoza   Merlo

Santiago   URUGUAY

Buenos Aires   Montevideo

Ruta 40

Zapala

Puerto Montt

Puyuhuapi

Villa O'Higgins

Tolhuin

Ushuaia

THE END OF THE WORLD

Cycling from Brazil to Tierra del Fuego

After three months, we take the panniers out of the large hatch at the front of the boat and lift the bikes off the deck. Anxiously, we tear the plastic off. We are afraid that everything will have rusted, but one brown chain link and a bent mudguard are the only damages after three months of salt and sunshine. Dieter and Margrit have never seen us on our bikes and look full of admiration as we get them in shape. Thanks to their generosity and kindness, we are on the other side of the Atlantic Ocean with our bicycles. Now we can return to our familiar routine, which is anything but familiar in a new country.

A Rusted Link

Riding Together Again through Brazil

A routine is useful until the situation changes. A new continent means new questions. How do we find a place to sleep here? What time does the sun set? Do Brazilians eat bread? Are the stores closed on Sunday? Yet it is mainly the uncomfortable environment—the heat, mosquitoes, tropical rains, and security—that forces us to adjust our routine.

We cycle from the marina to the suburbs of the city. Zoë is dead on her feet after only 100 meters. We have had virtually no exercise for months. It is barely 20 kilometers (12.5 miles) to our host's house, but we creep along at a snail's pace. At 6 p.m. nightfall begins and within 15 minutes it is completely dark. We are in the middle of a slum on our first night in Brazil—not the best start in a new country.

"Do we dare ask for directions here, or do we pretend it's perfectly normal that we're here?" Zoë asks with tension in her body. We look for the address of our host, who lives in a gated community. "According to the map it should be somewhere around here, but I doubt it," says Olivier as he looks up the address on his phone. All we see around us are decrepit houses. A man sees us and asks if we have lost our way. He gives us directions and quickly adds that it is not very smart to cycle here in the dark. "Tomorrow we'll start looking for a place to sleep earlier," declares Zoë.

I don't want to cycle anymore

Mixed feelings overwhelm us as we get back on our bikes. We are coming to grips with the sudden transition between our two worlds. Olivier said goodbye to sailing a month ago and is happy to be back on his familiar means of transport. For Zoë, the change feels too fast. The Atlantic crossing has taken its toll on her. She is physically weak and severely thin, but mentally it is even harder for her to adapt to the busy traffic and noisy streets. She wants to rest, sort out her thoughts, and process the arduous crossing. "I don't want to cycle anymore," she finally proclaims.

Olivier misunderstands and reacts angrily. "Why? We've only been here two days. Pull yourself together! What do you want—to go home? Travel by bus? Then I'll continue cycling alone!"

Zoë is homesick—not for home, but for love and a sympathetic ear. For four weeks her diary has been her best friend, but she is still full of bottled-up emotions. "I don't want to go home at all. I just want some peace and quiet."

"Why did you say you don't want to cycle anymore? That scares me," says Olivier who realizes he reacted harshly. "We'll take our time until your desire to travel returns."

He gives her a long hug. That's how it usually goes with us. The real solution is not fancy words but a genuine hug. Doubt isn't a bad thing at all. It is a signal telling us to think about what we truly want.

After two weeks of rest in Recife, Zoë's batteries are fully charged, and she has gained back some weight. She feels revived by love, peace, and rest. Now her addiction to adventure and physical challenge demands attention. We get on our bikes, and it feels like the world trip is starting all over again.

To be honest

After 1,000 kilometers (620 miles) along the Brazilian coast, we arrive in Salvador. We knock on the door of Adriana's beautiful house where we'll be staying for a few days. Before we know it, we are sitting down for dinner. When Adriana serves up the rice, she accidentally knocks off her fork, which flies through the air and lands on the floor. "Oops," she says and kicks the fork under the counter. We look at each other and try not to laugh.

We offer to cook for her the next evening. We buy ingredients at the supermarket and use a packet of spaghetti that we find in the cupboard. As Olivier serves up the food, Zoë suddenly notices a few black dots on the cooked pasta. "Oh no! Olivier, look—there are bugs in the food," Zoë says, startled.

By then, Adriana has joined us. "Just pretend everything is fine," Olivier whispers quickly in Dutch.

"I can't." Zoë pretends to have just discovered the bugs. "Oh no, look—there are bugs in the food."

"Really? Nooo?" Adriana seems unconcerned and starts eating. Zoë eats her plate but leaves all the black dots. Olivier dismisses them—they are just extra protein after all. But, while doing the dishes, he looks to see if the fork is still under the sink. "This is really nasty," Olivier gags as he lies on the floor. There are hundreds of white maggots crawling around under the cupboards.

Uncomfortable moments such as these happen regularly. In Alabama, we have a host who is an angry drunk two nights in a row. In Colombia, we are guests of two women whose floor is littered with dog poop. In Peru, we sit at a table with a pilot who smokes joints and gets angry because we don't believe the earth is flat.

In Texas, a man invites us to sleep in his house after meeting us in the park, but when his wife sees us, she is furious. It happens frequently that the unwitting partner needs a little time to get used to us strangers. Often it is the lady of the house who avoids eye contact with us and looks at her husband angrily. Things almost always work out but not with the woman in Texas. In fact, she was so angry with her husband that she packed her suitcase and went to sleep at her mother's house.

A situation is uncomfortable only when we are uncomfortable. If we are relaxed, so is the host. We act in an easy-going and familiar way. When an experience does cross our comfort boundaries, we address it. To the drunken host, Zoë said that she did not like his attitude. We asked Adriana if she knew that there were maggots under the sink. Then we cleaned the house together and cooked the rest of the days. Setting our own boundaries when we are guests is not easy but neither are maggots on the floor.

The historic center of Salvador is known for its colonial architecture with colorful houses and cobblestone streets (above). Day after day, we have flat tires. Close to Aracaju, we have used all our spare inner tubes, and the glue to repair tires doesn't hold in the heat. We are forced to take a bus, but it never comes (below).

Large flocks of scarlet ibises return home after a day of foraging. Thousands of birds color the sky and make the trees look adorned with ornaments (top). During the rainy season, the valleys among the dunes fill with freshwater lagoons in Lençóis Maranhenses National Park (opposite).

Local fishermen arrive back at their fishing camps on a small beach along the coast of north Brazil.

First aid

Our visas are still valid for one month, but the closest border is 3,000 kilometers (1,900 miles) away—much too far to cover by bicycle alone. We take the bus from Salvador to southern Brazil. Three days of looking out a window to travel months' worth of pedaling. After so many months on a sailboat, it is not a tough task. In fact, it is a pleasant ride. A Brazilian with angular features has been sitting next to us the entire trip. He is traveling alone but suddenly turns to the person behind him.

"I don't feel well," Olivier hears him say. Then his eyes roll back, and he collapses. Zoë jumps up and lays him flat across the seats. She pulls up his T-shirt and searches for his heart. Stay calm, she thinks. Just as she is to begin chest compressions, he suddenly begins to shake and gasp vigorously. His arms move back and forth spasmodically. He might choke, she thinks in panic.

When we started our trip we told Zoë's mother, "We don't need travel insurance. We're going to bicycle, and we'll be in great shape. Nothing will happen to us."

She shook her head. "You guys might be fit, but if we die suddenly, that's also an emergency for you."

Upon reflection, we realize that we were also naive to the potential risks we faced. Steve, a volunteer for the Search & Rescue team in Canada, confronts us with the truth again later in the trip. We are preparing for our long ski adventure and tell him we won't be taking a satellite messenger. "They can find you after two hours, or after a week. Think about the volunteers that are looking for you and your family back home," he says. "Do you really want to put other people at risk and cause unnecessary concern for your loved ones?"

Before we left the Netherlands, Zoë took a first aid and CPR course. All the exercises were done on a dummy, but now she is sitting on the bus with her hands on the chest of a stranger. His eyes open but then quickly close again. She puts her lips over his mouth. Both his breathing and heart rate are disturbingly low. She panics.

"Shit, shit, what was it, what do I have to do if his heart stops?" She tries to remember the rhythm. Okay, 30 to two, that's it, 30 chest compressions and two rescue breaths. Just as she's about to start, the spasm stops. He's breathing again. Zoë breathes a sigh of relief. Olivier finds the identity card in the man's backpack. His name is Marcus, but there is no medical information. The ambulance is on its way, but the nearest hospital is 200 kilometers (125 miles) out.

"Marcus, stay awake," Zoë says a hundred times as she squeezes his cheeks and puts wet wipes on his forehead. An hour and a half later the ambulance staff finally treats the man. The paramedic tells Zoë that Marcus might have died without her help.

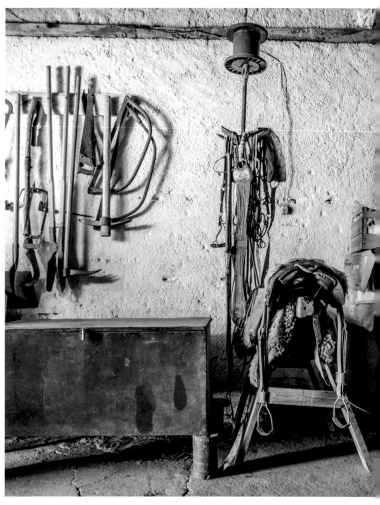

Paulo is a true gaucho, a traditional, skilled horseman of southern Brazil. The large piece of meat grills for six hours. It is only served on very special occasions—a huge compliment that our visit is one of those occasions.

We met Paulo at a horse race in Porto Alegre, the capital of the Brazilian state of Rio Grande do Sul. Paulo breeds race horses and has over 50 horses on his farm. At the age of 17, he became a jockey and was a professional for four years.

We know no strangers

Southern Brazil is wildly different than the north. There is more wealth, people have lighter skin, and it is cold in the winter. It is the right temperature to hunker down deep inside our down sleeping bags. We emerge from our bags in the morning with cold hands and noses. It's wonderful, it's perfect, and we enjoy it to the fullest. Each day we pack the tent and wave goodbye to any new friends, and by the evening, 80 kilometers (50 miles) later, we pick out a random house somewhere at the top of the next hill and ask for a safe spot in their yard.

Since our first day in Brazil, we have heard unpleasant stories about robberies, drugs, and murder. People keep saying it's unsafe "there" and point in the direction of an area. We feel anything but unsafe, but the words stick in the back of our minds. In our tent we cannot hide, so we are always looking for a safe haven with a stranger. "Never go with a strange man or woman," are the words we are taught at an early age. In southern Brazil, we do it all the time.

We knock on Maria Helena's door in hope of sleeping in her yard. She looks at us suspiciously and even angrily. "Can we pitch our tent in the garden?" we repeat because she may not have understood correctly. A strange smile appears, and we can tell she is thinking, "are you crazy?" as she waves us off toward the empty house across the street. We thank her kindly and sit on the little wall near the empty building. Soon Maria Helena comes back with two bananas and a can of Coke.

"You can sleep in the party room in the yard. It's dangerous outside," she says. We gratefully accept and settle ourselves in on the floor. Every half hour she finds an excuse to peep into the room. She comes and goes but never empty-handed or without an answer to a new question. She transforms from a frightened stranger to a warm hostess. She returns with bread, cookies, cheese, and milk. Later she brings pillows and towels, like a mother caring for her children. She says, "oh child, poor thing," when Zoë tells her that she took a sink bath.

The people who host us often ask, "Aren't you afraid that the people who invite you in might harm you?" We always answer with the question, "Aren't you afraid that we might rob your house?"

"What are you going to take?" one host says laughing. "The TV won't fit in your panniers."

The next morning Maria Helena knocks on the door with a tray in her hands. A little later we sit down for breakfast with *café da manhã*, chatting as friends. Later she waves goodbye and says she hopes that we find another safe haven with a stranger that evening.

An old car turned into an artsy planter in the streets of Colonia del Sacramento, one of the oldest towns in Uruguay (above).
Sheepskins drying on a clothesline in the pasture (opposite).

Among the Gauchos

Making Friends in Uruguay

An unfamiliar sound hovers over the undulating landscape. In fact, it is actually the absence of sound that abounds—complete silence. We move through a still life, gently rolling forward. The tick, tick, tick of our bike chains keep time like the second hand of a clock. We take a deep breath and exhale the hustle and bustle of Brazil that is evaporating into the tranquility of Uruguay. Gauchos color the landscape. They are descendants of Spaniards and Indigenous People who work on the cattle ranches in the Pampas of South America. Relaxed, they ride along to the rhythm of their horses as they trot through the Pampas. They tip their hats elegantly as we pass them. Their goodness is authentic, their lives rough, and their character conscientious.

In the open landscapes, wild camping doesn't seem to be a problem. However, on our first night in Uruguay, we choose a safe option and knock on the door of one of the few houses along the road. Inside, four people are sitting on simple plastic chairs near a crackling fireplace. Quickly they slide in two more chairs and seat us close to the fire.

"Mate?" the man next to Olivier asks, handing over a steaming mug. Mate is the typical tea in South America's southern countries. The tea, yerba mate, is mixed with hot water in a special round mug and drunk through a *bombilla,* a thick iron straw. The host continually refills the mug and it is passed around the table. Olivier speaks better Spanish and does the talking. Zoë speaks with her hands and her smile.

"She doesn't understand any of it, does she?" says Beatríz.

Zoë wants to protest and explain that she does understand, but she can't find the words. Beatríz lives in a large rectangular building that serves as the office for the local cattle auction once a month. The marketplace consists of a small arena where the cattle parades and buyers bid for the cows, horses, and sheep. We are allowed to sleep inside the office and, in the evening, join a hearty Uruguayan peasant meal.

"You keep eating but are so thin," she says and pouts her lips. We are given the nicknames *los dos flaquitos,* the two thin ones.

The next morning Beatríz waves goodbye to us with tears in her eyes. She promises Zoë that she's going to sell one of her cows to buy a bicycle. She wants to work on her health. A month later, we receive a message with a proud photo of her new bike, followed by updates on the weight she is losing.

Sheepskins are used to make saddles more comfortable. Horses are still the most common means of transportation for the gauchos in Uruguay (above). A gaucho is waiting for cattle to be loaded into a truck (opposite).

More friends

In Uruguay, wild camping isn't so easy after all. Most of the land is owned by large farms which are protected by fences. The owners usually live in the city and the farms themselves are inhabited and run by hard-working gauchos. When we ask one of them if we can camp in the fields, the answer is, "It's not my land; I have to ask *el patrón* for that, and he's not here. If I was the boss, you would be allowed to stay here," they often say, and we know they mean it.

With rosy cheeks from the cold, we stand at the gate of a remote farm. This one is our last hope before we have to pitch our tent next to the road. We wave from afar. A man approaches us, walking with a limp. Every step looks exhausting, and his right arm swings uncontrollably at his side. At the gate, Ruben greets us warmly in a Spanish we barely understand. He looks back and says we can stay the night, but also whispers, "The boss has just arrived. He only comes to visit once a month. Cycle on for a hundred meters, wait there, and come back when the car leaves." Feeling unsure, we do as he asks. We cycle on and hide behind a small hill. It is late and we are freezing cold. We don't know how long it will take and if we have understood him correctly. We mentally prepare for a freezing night next to the road.

Half an hour later, we are drinking mate with Ruben in the little kitchen next to the farm. We learn that a stroke has left him paralyzed on the right side of his body. He staggers around like a drunk and seems to lose his balance with every step. When he sits, his right arm rests on his lap, which suddenly gives him the appearance of a proper gentleman. "People from the city are afraid of strangers, but I have lived in the countryside for years and am still a free man," Ruben says proudly. We cook on his stove and sleep in *el patrón*'s bed. Meanwhile, he crawls under a thick blanket next to the fireplace.

A raid to remember

We deliberately choose to cycle through the interior of Uruguay, far from the busy roads along the coast. In search of local and authentic culture, we stumble upon an unusual horse racing competition—a raid. These are marathon races of at least 80 kilometers (50 miles) on public roads. Each jockey has a team car in which the whole family is crammed. In the cargo bed of the truck, there is a large water tank to cool the horse down during the race. The whole event is a bit like a cycling race and can even be followed live on radio and TV. The finish is packed with spectators.

After such a grueling race, the participants cross the finish line one by one. The horses are exhausted, and some jockeys have to move mountains to make the horse run the last 100 meters (110 yards). The next day we are invited to the awards ceremony where we join the gauchos for Uruguayan stew while the mate is passed from mouth to mouth.

Two gauchos vaccinate and brand their cattle. The branding iron is heated on a gas burner and used immediately on the hindquarters of the calves (opposite & top). A competitor in a raid, a traditional horse-racing competition (bottom).

Argentina's Vast Steppe

Cycling through the Pampas from East to West

At the Brazilian-Uruguayan border, we exchanged our last reals for Uruguayan pesos. We have experienced such generous hospitality that we are still carrying the same pesos from two weeks ago. It will be different in the big city, we think. We are on the ferry that will take us from Uruguay to Argentina. As all the drivers rush to their cars, we are already standing by our bikes. One man approaches us confidently. He looks friendly and asks in English where we are from. We answer in Spanish. His next question comes quickly and prepared.

"Do you already have a place to sleep in Buenos Aires?" We actually do but feel compelled to accept his invitation. Something in his directness makes us curious.

We immediately feel at home with Eduardo and Ili. Eduardo is a courteous man, very organized, and a bit authoritarian. He reminds Zoë very much of her father. They both served in the military and have the same passion for urban planning, geography, history, and art. Zoë's father likes to paint feminine curves, while Eduardo likes to creatively portray women with his camera. Ili works long hours, but when she comes home in the evening and we sit at the table together, all attention is on us. Dinner is family time, which reminds Olivier of his own home. Our new travel-parents' house becomes our home for a while. We stay a little longer, and they get to know us well and feel familiar. They literally replace the role of our own parents for a while. A smile, a pat on the back, a hug, and a sympathetic ear. Staying in a place where we feel at home gives us the space to recharge our batteries. We enjoy "normal" things like watching a movie on the couch at night and getting to know one place well. We become part of the family. We know their weekly schedule, we join them on family visits, we help out with chores around the house, and we can share our feelings with them.

In almost every country we meet new parents who take care of us like their own children. They are happy to have children in the house again for a while. On rare moments we really miss home.

The railway station in Buenos Aires, Argentina's capital (opposite). The first 600 kilometers (373 miles) after Buenos Aires, the land is completely flat and agriculture is dominant. From the San Luis Province, the mountains return and cycling becomes a lot more exciting (above).

Argentina was once one of the wealthiest nations in the world. Today, the economy is less prosperous. But some parts of Buenos Aires feel like the large avenues of New York City, with countless theaters and bookstores.

This usually happens when we hear about missed family events like Zoë's grandpa's birthday or Olivier's grandmother's funeral.

Eduardo reveals that he had been curious about us on the ferry. He heard us talking but wasn't sure of the language. Our clothing and the unfamiliar tongue had intrigued him. "You seemed like a nice couple and looked well behaved," says Eduardo. He had a week off and decided that he had both the time and space to help. His phone wasn't working, so he couldn't tell Ili that he wanted to invite us. It's now or never he thought when he saw us with our bikes. Once home, he told his wife, "Ili, I did something crazy. I invited a couple."

"Oh, are they coming for dinner this evening?" she asked.

"No, no, to stay for a few days," he said with a grin.

On the right track

We have 1,200 kilometers (750 miles) to go to Mendoza through vast lowland Pampas with monotonously flat terrain. The prospect is boring, but we want to try before we simply take the bus. The railroad tracks become our guide through the seemingly endless kilometers. The English engineers who came here to build the train network left their mark with town names like Carlos Keen, Open Door, and Wheelwright. The villages all have the same urban planning; they grow from the train station to a central square with a church and town hall. The wider circumference is flanked by miles of meadows and fields. The railroad may be dead, but we are transported like an invisible locomotive along the abandoned rails from one stop to the next. Before we leave one station, we already know the next. Our caring hosts provide new contacts down the line that offer us a warm place to stay every night.

On our next stop, Lito is our host. He pleasantly receives us but also seems hesitant. He isn't sure if it is such a good idea to open up his home because his son, Franco, has a slight disability and a hearing implant. However, we all get along so well that Lito realizes that the gamble was worth it. Together with Franco, we turn the house upside down with our fun and games. We play rugby and gossip about his secret love. Lito is so grateful to us that he signs up to become a Warmshowers host.

Pablo usually receives his guests on the lawn of the sports club. But when we arrive, he says it is too cold for a tent, and he invites us to his house. He has been hosting cyclists for several years. That same evening, the entire living room is filled with curious friends and family. Pablo takes us to his work. He is a veterinarian which is a very busy and important job on the Pampas. Angus steak is Argentina's main export, and he makes sure the cattle stay healthy.

Martin, an acquaintance of Pablo's, takes us to an auction at an affluent ranch in the area. There, the best cattle are presented complete with nameplates, which rate their health and breeding. Ranchers from all over the province come to bid on the animals. Ridiculous amounts are offered because everyone wants to produce and sell the best Angus steaks to Europe. The best cattle are sold for €15,000 ($16,000) a head.

Argentina is the fourth-largest beef producer in the world. The best cattle are sold at livestock auctions. A group of gauchos evaluates the cattle on offer (top). La Boca is one of the most popular neighborhoods in Buenos Aires and home to Boca Juniors, one of the two largest football teams in Argentina (opposite).

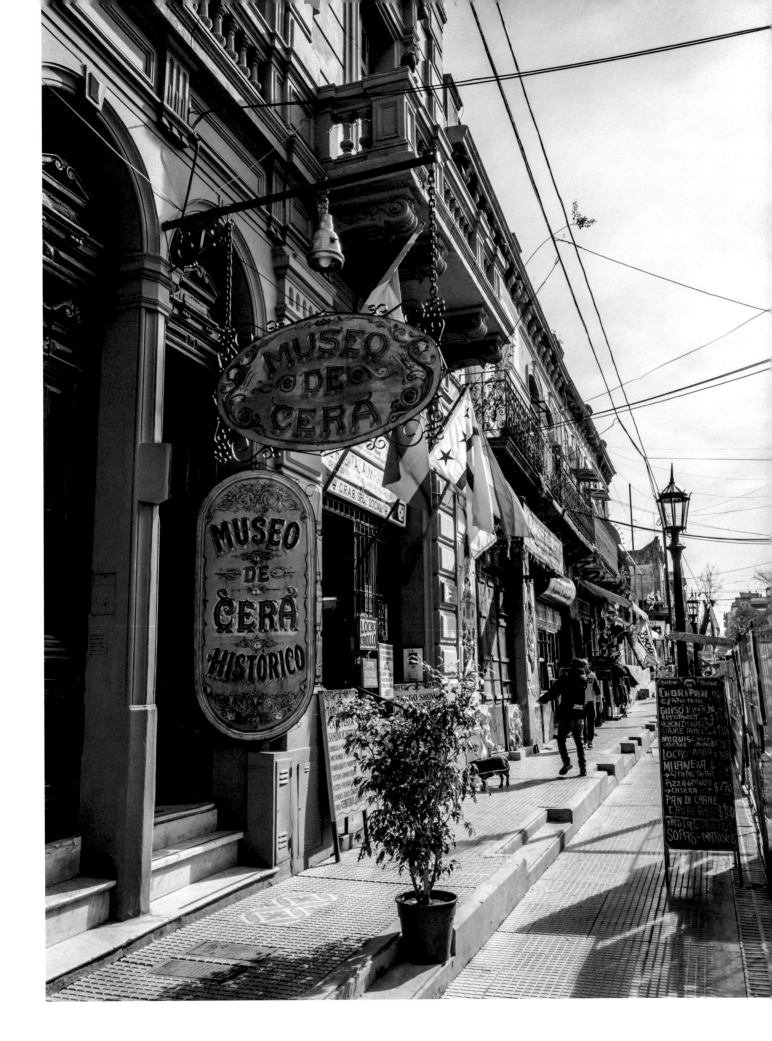

Choices

A man on a motorcycle stops and asks us if we already have a place to sleep for the night. He lives in the next village and invites us in. "If you win the game of pelota, we'll go flying tomorrow," Tatalo promises as we are sitting around his kitchen table. His hobby is flying light-sport aircrafts, and there are a few in the barn. The next day we fly in a 1946 Auster and briefly pilot the small plane ourselves.

As we ride further south, the flat Pampas gradually change to the hills of Cordóba. We are in the middle of the Argentinian winter, but we don't notice that very much. During the day, it is 25°C (77°F) with clear blue skies. Suddenly, we are almost in Mendoza. Everything seems perfect until we end up at a busy four-lane highway.

The road sign says that the speed limit is 100 kilometers per hour (62 miles per hour). Trucks pass way too close to us engulfing us in clouds of dust and fumes. We have some rules on the bicycle and one of them is that we don't cycle on highways. We see that detouring is not an option after looking at the map, and the next parallel road is 110 kilometers (68 miles) away. We pull over and—with a slight sense of disappointment—stick out our thumbs. Olivier begins taking the panniers off his bicycle, and before he has finished, a car has already pulled over. The disappointment quickly disappears when we are sitting comfortably in the back seat and telling our travel story to the curious driver. When we are almost there, he tells us that the parallel road is too bad for cycling and suggests dropping us off

A flamingo searches for food in one of the many lagoons high in the Andes Mountains (opposite). In northeastern Argentina, the gaucho culture makes way for the Andean culture.

20 kilometers (12.5 miles) further on. We agree but feel guilty that we are not moving under our own steam. On the horizon, the first peaks of the Andes appear.

A tear rolls down the corner of Olivier's eye but not from joy. Zoë looks aside and bites her lip. She knows it, and she feels the same. We had been looking forward to this moment for ten months. We have been cycling toward the Andes for almost a year, waiting for this moment. Now we see it not from our bikes but through the window of a car.

We decide to bike back to the beginning of the bad road, perhaps hoping to feel what we wanted to feel. The next day the Andes reappear, but the special moment has already been stolen. "At least we learned that cycling back is an idiotic idea," says Zoë.

At Daniel's house, we are preparing for the 4,000-kilometer (2,500-mile) stretch to Ushuaia. All our gear, including ourselves, is getting refurbished. New tires and cassettes are fitted on our bikes, our clothes are sewn, and our hair is cut. We plan routes and write messages to Warmshowers hosts. Ruta 40 is known for its high winds and long stretches of unpaved roads. We will be entering a desolate area with huge distances between basic amenities. We feel well prepared, but we are not quite sure what to expect on our next adventure. Can we and our retro bicycles handle it? We buy food for the first four days because we know we won't find anything for the next 270 kilometers (168 miles).

We don't get off to a good start. A fierce wind blows in our faces. The sandy road is soft and turns into a bumpy washboard. Our good spirits take a serious hit. The sand gets looser, the rocks bigger, and the wind blows harder by the minute. Soon we can't cycle anymore, and we are forced to push our bikes. We barely cover 3 kilometers (2 miles) in an hour. Zoë's face speaks volumes, and Olivier becomes distant. He responds gruffly. "Stop!" he says. "We won't make it. If the road stays like this, we won't have enough food. We have to go back and detour on the main road."

Back on the paved road, the wind blows devastatingly. It is snowing and hailing. We barely move forward. The wind gusts batter against our panniers and sides. We push our handlebars in the right direction, but the wind picks us up and drags us to the other side of the road. Olivier needs all his strength to stay on his feet.

"This is extremely dangerous," Zoë yells. "We have to keep going," Olivier shouts back. "There's no other option!" There are no houses or trees to protect us from the wind. All we can do is keep going and hope that we find shelter. Our salvation is a small wooden house that has miraculously survived the force of the wind. Outside, a goat's head is hanging on the clothesline. Blood is slowly dripping on the ground. The old woman immediately calls us inside and ladles out a hot goat stew. We warm up and mentally recharge ourselves to continue after lunch. Our basic needs have been replenished for a while, thanks to this unexpected hospitality on the endless steppe.

Just across the border of Chile, in the Atacama Desert, lies Valle de la Luna (Moon Valley). The stone and sand formations have an impressive range of colors and textures that resemble the surface of the moon.

The Andes is the dividing line between Chile and Argentina, perhaps one of the most beautiful borders in the world.
Las Piedras Rojas (Red Stones) are only on the Chilean side.

Laguna de los Tres is a popular hike around Argentina's most famous mountain, Fitz Roy (above). Endless windswept roads along the Andes offer majestic views and tough days on the bike (opposite).

Suffering on Ruta 40

In the Desolate Wilderness of Patagonia

A Patagonian storm blows us off the road with hail and sand pelting our faces. Yesterday the fire department told us to get off the street. "Too dangerous to be outside," they said. Mentally we are testing our limits, but there are people who always live in these harsh conditions.

Dogs bark as we approach the property. Gaucho Dario is anything but surprised when he sees us and our bikes. He and his brother are the youngest in a family of 10 and are the only ones left to take care of their family home. The three small houses form the only settlement in the area. Dario's wife is about to give birth and has been in town with their two daughters for several days.

Camping is almost impossible with these gusts. Out of necessity, we end up pitching in the gutter of the road a few times, where we have just enough protection from the wind. Dario drives his tractor out of the garage, and we pitch the tent under the corrugated metal roof. Windswept, we come in for a hot mate. The house is unusually simple and orderly. Every object is useful, and everything has its place. The mate is poured with

elegance and the *bombilla* is carefully cleaned after each sip. He has no electricity, so there is no refrigerator, telephone, or washing machine. He has a solar panel that provides just enough electricity to power the light. Dario talks about his simple living conditions. Every morning he looks for his goats on the ridge. He says the climate has changed extremely. There used to be snow in winter, which made for a green pasture, but now everything is dry and barren. He has to go high up into the mountains to find fresh grass for the goats. When we tell him that the changes also affect us, he replies with his calm voice, "Aha, climate change is happening on a global scale." Amazed, he tries to imagine how we can live in such a small country like the Netherlands or Belgium, while he leans back crossing his legs.

Dario gives us strength in the harsh world of the Argentine steppe. His happiness with a simple and uncertain lifestyle is admirable. Just as people are amazed that we cycle here, we are amazed that he lives here. Attitude is everything. "Today we'll beat the wind," Zoë says triumphantly as we jump on our bikes.

Los Caracoles Pass, the Snail's Pass, is a series of beautiful hairpin curves on the road from Zapala to Junín de los Andes. Down in the valley, Rio Aluminé gives us an abundance of water and greenery after weeks of arid landscapes.

Can we talk?

The landscape is rough, brown, and barren. Zoë cycles behind Olivier on autopilot lost in thought. "What are you thinking about?" she asks when we have been cycling for an hour without saying a word.

"Nothing," says Olivier. "What do you mean, nothing?" Zoë asks. "Just, nothing, no idea."

"You have to be thinking about something," she says, slightly irritated.

Zoë's mind never stops jumping from one thought to another. She can see a flower beside the road and recall a vacation in France, which reminds her of a movie she saw with a friend, that makes her think back to high school and the French exam where she secretly cheated. To organize her thoughts, Zoë's mother told her to imagine her head as a cabinet with individual compartments that she can open, put her thought in, and then close again. In vain, her brain looks like a satellite image of the earth at night—a fascinating network of light interconnected to each other. Memories and emotions are linked everywhere.

Zoë's mother's cabinet seems to be in Olivier's head. He has a drawer for every part of his life that he can pull open and use at the right time. When he opens drawers while cycling, it is usually for practical things. Where should we refill our water? How much food do we have left? Or he calculates the average

speed based on the kilometer signs next to the road. More often than not, his drawers are completely closed, and he isn't thinking about anything—much to Zoë's frustration.

Before setting out, Zoë's biggest fear was that we wouldn't have anything to say to each other after weeks on the road. As it turns out, the opposite is true. There is so much to talk about. The landscape that changes, the family who we stayed with, or yesterday's challenges (which are never that bad in retrospect). We dream, brainstorm, evaluate, and laugh on our bikes. Sometimes we are silent for hours and only talk during breaks. Sometimes we can't talk. Sometimes we don't want to talk and are deliberately silent. Sometimes we have to talk to argue or get something off our chests.

Making decisions together

We choose a beautiful route along the Laguna Blanca National Park. Actually, "choose" is perhaps not the right word. At the junction where the route turns right, we stand still for half an hour, arguing and shouting at each other.

"We're cycling straight up to the mountains, that's against the wind. Do you want that?" Olivier checks.

"I don't care; I'm just pedaling," says Zoë. "Go the way that you want."

A local fisherman tries to catch trout in Lago Nahuel Huapi, the largest lake in Argentina's Lake District (opposite). Early October, spring is coming, but there is still snow in the mountains (above).

Perito Moreno is one of the 48 glaciers fed by the Southern Patagonian Ice Field. The terminus of the glacier is 5 kilometers (3.1 miles) wide. Large chunks of ice break off at the terminus all the time, but the most spectacular event is the rupturing of a giant ice bridge, which happens every few years.

"Nonsense, when we're 15 minutes down the road, you'll be irritated and say that we should have taken the other route."

Okay, we'll take this route. No, because of this and that. Yes, but... It goes on like this for half an hour until we are so frustrated with each other that we refuse to speak at all. Finally, we choose a route and promise each other that we'll stop whining. But, we know we can do better than that.

"I have an idea," says Zoë, "about how we can make better decisions together."

It's not about the simple choices, like do we eat pasta with cream or tomato sauce, but about the decisions where we really have to consider our options. For us, it is usually decisions like route choice, spending our travel budget in a restaurant, or whether to take a rest day that cause us to start arguing.

Zoë quickly comes up with a proposal, "We take ten minutes and make a choice for ourselves. Then we tell each other about the choice. It is important, though, that we choose for ourselves and not just to accommodate the other."

"Sounds good, but if we have opposite opinions, what then?" Olivier thinks aloud.

"Well, then after careful consideration, we explain why we think so," says Zoë.

That last thing turns out to be the key to our success. Two things happen. First, we learn how the other person thinks, and why he or she wants something. Second, we become convinced by the other person's argument, or we find out that our own argument isn't so strong after all. Thus, we arrive at a mutual decision without arguing. This successful formula has never failed! The hardest part is recognizing that we are thinking about a "decision."

Back in Argentina and after half an hour, Olivier suddenly stops and gets off the bike. He steps up to Zoë and gives her a hug. "Sorry, Zoë." "Sorry for what?" she asks. "Just sorry, no explanation," says Olivier. "I was wrong too, sorry. Let's not argue about such silly things," suggests Zoë.

There is hardly any traffic, we hardly feel any headwind, and the white peaks of the Andes are so beautiful. "If I had known this, we would have turned right immediately," says Olivier.

Camping at the shore of Laguna Torre offers a spectacular view of Cerro Torre. Mount Fitz Roy is a popular destination for climbers. It's extremely technical and difficult to traverse the whole range.

Carretera Austral

The Only Way South

We have been looking forward to the Carretera Austral for a long time. The route is often touted as a "not-to-be-missed" long-distance route. It is the only road in Chilean Patagonia. The route starts in Puerto Montt and ends 1,240 kilometers (771 miles) south in Villa O'Higgins. After that, there is only wild nature and icy landscapes. The route runs parallel to Ruta 40 but on the Chilean side of the Andes. It is known for its beautiful landscapes but also unpaved roads, remote villages, and lots of rain. We like it better than the dry Pampas and wind of the past few weeks, but we are still a bit apprehensive about the many kilometers on dirt roads. Fifty years ago, there were no roads at all. "There was absolutely nothing here—no streets, no electricity, just a few houses," Padre Antonio tells us.

That afternoon we knocked on the church door, and to our surprise, the pastor said, "*We kunnen gewoon Nederlands praten*" (We can just speak Dutch). His real name is Toon van Kessel and he arrived in Chile on a cargo ship about 50 years ago. Many missionaries had come before him but few stayed long. He did not give up. Even though he started out as an unknown stranger, he has become a national hero. He brought electricity, taught sewage treatment techniques, and built thirty wooden churches by hand. His life motto, *la aventura recompensa la fatiga*— overcome fatigue with adventure—becomes our inspiration on the long stretches of unpaved roads.

Patrick on tour

Together with our Belgian companion Patrick, we enjoy the last stretches of asphalt along the Carretera Austral. Patrick is a tall, slender man with a tanned face and round glasses whose clothes betray the fact that he has been on the road for a while and has lost a few pounds since he started his bike trip. Our rhythms match perfectly. Our budget, on the other hand, is on a completely different level.

Patrick is a successful businessman with a generous budget, while ours is more modest. Depending on availability and his daily needs, he regularly chooses a hotel over his tent. Patrick is very curious about how we find a place to stay every night.

"I want to experience that. Can I join you tonight?" he asks. We take Patrick on our daily "evening tour." It's windy and the dark clouds are foreboding. We aim for a roof to put the tent under and begin our search in a small village. We ask if there is a fire station, look for the police station, walk into gymnasiums, and knock on church doors. We look for the boss, key holder, or owner of a building. Most times a name comes up, which is the clue to solving the puzzle. Today Mina has the key to the church, and she knows a good spot. She takes us to an old outbuilding next to the church.

When none of the keys seem to fit, she says, "Just break down the door." "No no, that's not necessary," Zoë says. "We can put the tent there too," and we point to a roof that is part of the church. She insists, "No, no, the door has to be opened sometime anyway". A little uncomfortably and in full sight of the road, Patrick and Olivier pry the lock off the door with all sorts of tools. Mina looks on approvingly and tells us that no one has been inside for at least two years.

We prepare ourselves for the worst when the door creaks open and are a bit afraid that it is too basic for Patrick. The four of us stand in the doorway looking inside. A festively decorated two-year-old withered Christmas tree gives the place an unexpected homey feel. There is a simple wooden board table, a few old chairs in a circle, and pictures of Jesus and Mary on the wall that seem to watch over us. We are pleased to see a wood-burning stove in the corner, which is enough to convince us over the threshold.

"Feel at home," says Mina and then disappears. We sweep the layer of dust off the floor and feel lucky to have such a nice place for the night. We light the wood-burning stove and drink hot chocolate while our pans simmer on the fire. Patrick seems to be enjoying himself which makes us happy too. It is nice to share our adventures and "tricks" with someone else.

"Nothing can spoil this day now," Patrick says before dozing off.

10,000 kilometers

In the last 200 kilometers (125 miles) of the Carretera Austral, we are faced with the desolate wilderness that epitomizes Patagonia. It is altogether rougher with robust vegetation that can withstand the harsh forces of nature. The route winds through the mountains which are covered with a thick snowpack. Amenities

Behind every bend is a new spectacular view of snowcapped mountains, glaciers, and blue-green rivers. At Mirador Cerro Castillo, we are blessed with sunny weather and a beautiful view of the Cerro Castillo mountain peak.

are nonexistent until the very end. There is hardly anyone who wants to live so far from civilization, but there are also people who feel at home here.

In the morning, we meet two Austrian cyclists, Bernd and Bernard. We decide to cycle together. We cycle for hours against the wind on a bad dirt road with loose gravel. Finally, we all decide it's time to find a camping spot, and we start looking around. Surprisingly, we spy a small house on the right-hand side of the road. It stands out because of the glare of the metal walls. A narrow chimney protrudes from the roof spewing out white smoke, and a Chilean flag flies on a long pole.

"Shall we?" asks Zoë when we see a man saddling up his horse. Like all the gauchos we meet, Erasmo is elegantly dressed. He wears neat jeans tucked into his leather boots. Under his knit vest, he wears a red shirt with rolled-up sleeves. He has muscular arms, a healthy tan, and a slightly graying mustache. He wears a Basque beret and a red scarf tied around his neck. The ruggedness of the landscape contrasts starkly with his kind demeanor, neat clothes, and charming smile.

Bernd and Bernard stand behind us and follow everything curiously. We act as experienced guides when it comes to finding a place to sleep. Erasmo invites us in for hot mate and points to the places where we can pitch the tent. Inside, it is orderly with lots of old stuff and canned food. The curtains are neatly tied back,

there is an old tablecloth on the wooden table, and a black kettle is boiling on the wood-burning stove in the corner. An old radio that Erasmo uses to communicate with the other gauchos in the area is hanging from one of the kitchen cabinets. We cook pasta, while Erasmo saws a piece of dried cow rib and seasons the pasta. He tells wild tales of pumas and hard winters. Bernd and Bernard barely speak a word of Spanish, but their Austrian sausage and whiskey only make Erasmo's storytelling more spectacular.

"*Salud!*" we toast for the fifth time that night.

"10,000 kilometers!" shouts Zoë and tilts her head back, downing another shot of whiskey. Olivier does the same and shouts, "Up to the next 10,000!"

We don't like strong alcohol at all, but Bernd and Bernard don't care about that. The two doctors are cycling the Carretera Austral together. For them, the bike ride is a three-week vacation, and they want to make the most of it. Together we reach Villa O'Higgins, the absolute end of the Carretera Austral and the road in southern Chile. For Bernd and Bernhard, it's another good reason to party. To thank us for the unforgettable experience at Erasmo's house, they give us the primary bedroom in a four-person cabin. In the evening we toast some more, this time with schnapps, then sing along to Bob Dylan and dance salsa on the table. The adult frat house parties on until the last candle has burned out.

A giant iceberg drifts on one of the lakes in Torres del Paine National Park (opposite). Puerto Río Tranquilo is a favorite stop for every traveler on the way south—not because of the town but the beautiful marble caves (above).

The farther south, the more remote the Carretera Austral becomes. The last 600 kilometers (375 miles) the road is unpaved. After Lago General Carrera, the largest lake in Chile, there is only one more town until the end of the road.

Our most remarkable border crossing

Zoë's father regularly told us exciting stories about the adventures of his youth. Forty years ago, he bought an old car in the southern United States. Together with a friend, he drove through Mexico and Central America. The border crossings were always challenging. They often had to put a stack of pesos into their passports to "keep them out of trouble." We regularly expect such problems in South America, but we never have to bribe anyone. On the contrary—at every border crossing, the customs officers have been more interested in our journey than our belongings. They take selfies with us, and they regularly offer us a place to sleep. The border we are about to cross between Chile and Argentina is exclusively for cyclists and there is no road, only a mountain pass.

On the map, the road stops after Villa O'Higgins, but cyclists and hikers know that there is a route beyond that. Other cyclists describe the crossing as emotional, grueling, or the hardest thing they have ever done. To get there, we first have to take a ferry across a long lake. Due to bad weather, the ferry hadn't sailed for several days, and there is a group of cyclists that has grown day by day. Besides our Austrian friends and Patrick, we see many familiar faces from the road. Among the group we spot "the Brazilian with the small dog," "Ross, the cyclist with the crazy hair," "the man with the trailer," and "Jean, the cyclist with the green bags." Finally, the weather eases and we all make the crossing on a tiny ferry.

The first kilometers we can ride, but soon we are off our bikes crossing rivers and wading through mud. We push the bikes up steep slopes, drag them over tree trunks, and slide through

Close to the small town of Puyuhuapi is the Ventisquero Colgante, the hanging glacier from which one of the highest waterfalls in South America emerges (opposite). Meeting a Chilean gaucho on the road, each amazed by the other's means of transportation (above).

narrow gullies where the bikes barely fit through. It's physically demanding. Lifting, pulling, and pushing—but it's pure fun. After every curve, a new obstacle awaits. Sometimes they seem unsurmountable, and we search for a more accessible route. Every cyclist goes through the course at his or her own pace. We stay with Patrick and have endless respect for this 63-year-old man. Five hours later, we plop the bike in the grass at Lago Desierto and see Fitz Roy rising mightily on the other side. The border post is a small hut with one table and two chairs. With the most cursory of inspections, we get the Argentina stamps in our passports.

A cemetery for cyclists

We are back in the dry landscape of Argentina. The wind determines our pace toward Ushuaia. We keep in close contact with all our cycling friends who are riding in front or behind us. Along the way, we pass iconic sleeping spots. But since we have a destination in mind, we roll past them. We all have the same goal—to cross the next finish line in Ushuaia.

We have to cross the Patagonian steppe to the Atlantic Ocean. It's a 450-kilometer (280-mile) stretch of desert-like plains. Several Argentines warned us. "There is nothing, but really nothing," and "It is a cemetery for cyclists." In theory, the wind is always blowing from the mountains to the coast, but that's only a theory. We fly out of El Chaltén on a pleasant tailwind that lasts for nearly 90 kilometers (55 miles), but then we get a strong side wind. We need to cycle 130 kilometers (80 miles) to the only wind-protected place, a pink house along the road. It is an abandoned restaurant that has become a well-known overnight stop for cyclists. There are no windows or doors, but the place is kept alive by cyclists. The walls are filled with messages from all the tired-legged, like-minded souls.

We leave at 5 a.m. to outwit the wind, but it gets its revenge later in the day. Weary, we choose a spot in the gutter to take a break from the wind.

"How is it possible!" Zoë says. She holds up a titanium fork, which can only be the remnant of some poor windblown cyclist's destruction. While moving, we rarely see other cyclists, but we know they are there. When we stop, it is a different matter. It's logical that we all find the same place to sleep, but the wind is such an enemy that we even descend on the same lunch spots.

We are only 100 kilometers (62 miles) from the finish line, and another icon is waiting for us. The bakery in Tolhuin is the overnight stop where cyclists leave in the morning with a bag full of yesterday's pastries. We meet "Ross, the cyclist with his crazy hair" again. He has already crossed the finish line and is hitchhiking his way north.

"Was it special arriving in Ushuaia?" Zoë asks in anticipation. "You know, it's just another city. After so many finished destinations, it's just one out of many," he responds.

Eventually, the gates of Ushuaia welcome us too. Beyond them lies a city much larger than the idyllic idea of the end of the world. Large factories line the outskirts of the city, cruise ships bound for Antarctica fill the harbor, and the mountainsides are speckled with houses. For our cycling friends, Ushuaia is the final destination of a long journey. We are relieved that we are not going home yet. For us, this finish line is just one out of many at the end of the world but still special.

Les Eclaireurs Lighthouse stands in the Beagle Channel close to Ushuaia. In Argentina, it is also known as the lighthouse at the end of the world (opposite). Large colonies of sea birds, penguins, and walruses live on the islands in the Beagle Channel (above).

We have to force ourselves to slow down and enjoy the beautiful camping spots along the Carretera Austral, like here along Lago General Carrera.
Wild camping is the only option, but it's so easy here.

A Safe Place Every Night

Wild Camping and the Quirky Places We Slept

Sleeping in villages

The smaller the village, the easier it was to find a place. In larger cities, we never tried. We always said that it was only for one night. We never just pitched our tent in a village. We always asked for permission. That way people knew who we were and trusted us. We always said goodbye and left a postcard to thank them.

On people's property

We asked people who were outside. We only ever rang doorbells to ask for water. Preferably, we asked farmers because they have a lot of land. We introduced ourselves and were direct in our questioning: "Can we pitch our tent in your yard? Tomorrow we will continue." If we didn't speak the language, we wrote those simple sentences on a piece of paper.

Public places or institutions

We have slept in churches, parks, playgrounds, schools, sports fields, libraries, town halls, health centers, museums, and community centers. We usually avoided locations where children play or people walk in the evening.

In Latin America, the fire department often helped with shelter. The police and the army were usually too rigid. Our bicycles were often key to finding a place to sleep. These pieces of steel with four panniers had a special appeal. Without panniers, we would have been anonymous. When we arrived in a small village at the end of the afternoon, our search for a place to sleep began. We looked for a church, the town hall, or the local fire department. A guard often welcomed us and called his boss to ask permission. If the boss couldn't see our bikes, the power of persuasion was gone.

Strangest places slept

1. Airplane hangar – Spain
2. Army base – Guatemala
3. Bus shelter – Chile
4. Choza, a shepherd's hut made of straw – Ecuador
5. Our self-built igloo – Canada
6. Courtroom – Mississippi, USA
7. Salt restaurant – Argentina
8. Truck trailer – Argentina
9. Salt flats – Bolivia
10. Abandoned police station with an earthquake at night – Ecuador

Wild Camping

During the four years of our journey, we camped in almost every conceivable location; we slept in forests, fields, parks, squares, and on the side of the road. There were plenty of times when it wasn't possible to ask the owners' permission. In those situations, we considered it "wild camping."

How do we find a spot?

Apps like iOverlander, Park4Night, as well as government websites and interactive maps, are good tools for finding a spot. We also used our maps and GPS. We would search for lakes, rivers, hiking trails, parks, and dead ends. Forests are more difficult for wild camping than it seems. Steep slopes, vegetation, and critters were often our opponents.

Local knowledge

Locals knew the area better than we did, but asking for advice was rarely worthwhile. People think of hotels and campsites as places to stay, so rarely suggest good wild spots. To try and get around this, we would ask, "Is there a river or lake where we can pitch the tent?" or, "Do you think we can camp in that field?"

The perfect spot is ...

- Out of sight. We preferred a spot out of sight, without light or noise pollution. A lot of land is private property. So, when in doubt, we asked the owner if it was okay for us to stay overnight. If that wasn't possible then being out of sight was especially important.
- Sheltered from the elements. Do we want sun or just more shade? Evening sun or morning sun? Can we stay dry here if the weather changes?
- Flat. We needed an area big enough to pitch our tent that wasn't on a slope and didn't have any sharp protrusions.
- Insect free. We searched for signs of life on the ground and paid particular attention to lines in the grass or sand. This was where ants walked at night, and they could bite their way through the tent.
- Free of other natural dangers. We would check for dead branches above camp and knock them down.
- Close to water for cooking and washing. But is the site in a hollow that could pool rainwater in a storm? Could the river's water level rise at night? From which direction is the rain likely to come?
- Not too windy. Sometimes we wanted a breeze to escape from the mosquitoes, but other times we wanted more shelter against the wind.

Making do

We would start our search at least two hours before it got dark. It wasn't always easy, but we always found a spot. However, the reality is that there were more ugly camping spots than beautiful ones. We often ended up near a road, behind gas stations, or in abandoned parking lots. At night we could often hear cars pass and sometimes felt trucks rumbling by as we lay in our tent. Yet, once we were securely zipped in our tent, we made every spot our home.

The most important rule

We always made sure we left no trace. The only sign of us being at a sight was some flattened grass where our tent had been. We cleaned up everything, including other people's trash. We buried our human waste and carried out our toilet paper in a paper bag. We put everything back the way we found it, didn't use soap when washing in rivers or lakes, and never pitched our tent on fragile soils or plants.

Medellín

■ Bogotá

Cali

COLUMBIA

Pasto

ECUADOR

Quito

Máncora

PERU

Huaraz

Huánuco

Lima ■

Ayacucho

Cuzco

BOLIVIA

La Paz

Santa Cruz

Salar
de Uyuni

Villamontes

BRAZIL

PARAGUAY

Asunción

CHILE

ARGENTINA

URUGUAY

Buenos Aires ■

Ushuaia

FOLLOWING THE ANDES

Heading North to Columbia

It is Boxing Day, and we are at the airport in Ushuaia waiting patiently in the arrival area for the sliding doors to open. It has been exactly one year since we saw Olivier's parents. World travelers used to be unreachable and far away from family, but the distances that were once unbridgeable now have an occasional one-second delay on the phone line, and the other side of the world is only a flight away.

Far from Family

Resting and Recharging Our Batteries in Ushuaia

Having our family visit is like a short vacation from our long journey. We leave our bikes behind for a while. We proudly show our family where we sleep and which routes we have taken as well as how well we know the country, people, and local dishes. They go canoeing with us, hike through the snow, and sleep in mountain huts. They push their limits for us.

"Without you, we would never have traveled this far. Our world has become bigger and smaller at the same time," Olivier's mother tells us afterward.

Throughout our whole journey, our bond with our parents has grown. At home, we visited them once a month and stayed maybe one night. Now we call weekly and send a message every day. The contact is much more intense. "We see you less, but we know you much better," Olivier's father says.

Zoë's parents are less convinced. Although they are seasoned travelers, they miss sitting together in the living room. Our current conversations often revolve around our travels, experiences, and encounters. The journey is our life, and it is far from the life they live. They get much more information than before, but our phone calls rarely evolve into meaningful or philosophical discussions. They hear us more, but our conversations lack depth. One-second delay or not, a phone call can't replace the intimacy of the living room.

Home to roost

When Olivier's parents leave for Belgium, we rent a small room in Ushuaia for two months from an Argentine woman. Its modest furnishings—a double bed, small closet, and desk—barely fit in the room, but for us, it's enough. And at eight euros a day, we stay well within our travel budget. We don't have any new plans yet, just a lot of ideas. It is time for some rest and reflection. We put a large sheet of paper on the floor. Zoë writes "WeLeaf future" in the middle and says, "Go ahead." Soon the whole paper is full, and our next plans are clear.

The Argentine woman goes on vacation for a few weeks and entrusts us with the entire house. We receive her Airbnb guests and take care of the house. "My parents live next door, should there be any problems," she says.

That same afternoon we knock on her parents' door to introduce ourselves. A warm smell of oven-fresh empanadas wafts through the keyhole. Jorge and Marta—whom we are soon calling grandma and grandpa—welcome us into their tidy home. Jorge is a neat, polite, intelligent man and extremely curious. Marta is a true grandma who spoils us as if we were her grandchildren. She slides a warm empanada onto our plate, followed by a second and third. "I knew you would miss us," grandma says when we visit them later in the week.

From that moment on, they take us everywhere, making up new places to see every time. They confide in us that they would have liked their children's choices to be different. They should have gone to college instead of having children first. It is equally heartwarming and heartbreaking when they say they see us as their children. On their 49th wedding anniversary, they invite us out for dinner.

After two months of brainstorming, resting, writing, and studying, we get our bikes out of the garage. The new plans are clear, our brains rested, and our batteries recharged. Within an hour, everything is back in the same familiar place in our panniers. The busy highway on the windy east coast of Argentina is too dangerous to cycle, so we will have to find a ride for the next stretch. We cycle to the edge of town and start hitchhiking at the side of the road—destination Buenos Aires. "To the north," says Olivier.

Manuel

Manuel is kind enough to stop for us, and we jump aboard his truck. He and his friends take us all the way from Ushuaia to the border with Paraguay. The distance is 4,000 kilometers (2,485 miles), which is the same as a free ride from Madrid to Moscow.

"Feel at home and make yourself comfortable," Manuel says as we climb into the truck. There is a passenger seat and a sofa bed for the driver in the back. Water bottles, a teapot, and cookies fill the space between the passenger and the driver. Olivier starts on the bed, Zoë in the passenger seat.

Manuel transports cars from Buenos Aires to all corners of Argentina. He lives on the road. His truck is his home away from home. He visits his real home, where his wife and children live, once a week. We drive 20 hours a day, stopping occasionally for a little break. Manuel defies our stereotypical expectations of what a trucker is like. He doesn't burp, fart, or spew sexist remarks. Instead, he is a polite man with a playful sense of curiosity and a neat truck. We keep him company continuously. At night, we roll out our sleeping mats at the back of the empty trailer for a few hours of sleep.

Bicycles Go Too Fast

Unknown Paraguay

Five days of trucking sounds like an eternity, but on a bicycle, it would have taken us two months to cover the same distance. It feels like we are at the border of Paraguay in the blink of an eye. Along the way, we have spoken only to our driver, Manuel, and have met no one else. The environment has changed completely, and we barely noticed. We left the cold of the south and only learned in short stops that the temperature has risen. Our air-conditioned bodies still need to acclimatize. A humid, tropical heat welcomes us when we take the bikes off the trailer, wave goodbye to Manuel, and cycle to the border post. Our ears and eyes also have a lot to deal with. The customs officer speaks Spanish, but we don't understand a word. Our ears haven't had the time to learn the new accent. Besides Spanish, Paraguay has a second official language, Guaraní. Almost everyone in Paraguay speaks a mixture of both. People's skin is a shade darker, the houses are more colorful, and there are tropical plants in the yards. We realize the value of our usual slow mode of transportation in which we can feel, smell, hear, and see the environment. And sometimes we even think that our bicycles go too fast.

Food poisoning

Olivier leans limply over the toilet seat. He doesn't even have the energy to sit upright. His face is pale, and his forehead is beaded with sweat. It is March 30th, Good Friday, and just a few hours ago we were cycling through the streets with balloons on our bicycles. The past few days, we have been stopped at least 10 times for photos, drinks, or corn cookies, but today the streets are empty because everyone in Paraguay celebrates at home.

Cycling on red soil in the humid and subtropical east side of Paraguay (opposite). The west side of Paraguay has vast differences in water availability. During the rainy season, there is an excess of water and an abundance of green (above).

The restaurants and stores are even closed. We weren't prepared for this and searched hopelessly for a place to have lunch. Finally, we found a small store that was open. It had a few hamburgers and croquettes under a glass bell jar on the counter. "I'm not allowed to cook on Good Friday, so these are from yesterday," the woman explained as she pointed to the food.

We eat everything. Food has become something we put in our mouths to give us energy. We are used to the taste and smell of stale bread, sweaty cheese, hair in our food, chicken legs in our soup, flies buzzing around our ears, or someone nibbling a chicken neck next to us. Our stomachs don't care, as long as they get nutrition. We take the hamburger and the croquette. When Zoë sees the contents of the croquette, she won't eat it, but Olivier is always up for something new.

Now, Olivier hugs the toilet. To make matters worse, it's his thirtieth birthday. Olivier loses his appetite for a week and suffers from a grumbling stomach for the rest of our time in South America. Luckily, it remains the only time in our four-year journey that we get food poisoning. Everywhere we go we keep trying new things. It's part of our discovery. But a croquette in Paraguay? Never again!

A Belgian dinner

A few days later, we search for some familiar comfort food. We know that several Belgian families have lived in this part of Paraguay for more than 50 years, and we search with our noses for the familiar smell of fries and waffles. We find Erica, and she tells us her husband's life story: It is the winter of 1953 in Flanders.

El Chaco has a very low population density, and there are only a few towns. Filadelfia, in the center of El Chaco, was founded by Mennonites and is now an important cattle and dairy production center.

Children in a local school in Paraguay are very interested in our bicycles, the money we use, and where we sleep.

Carolus is 23 and wants to be a farmer, but there's hardly any land available. In the newspaper, there is an advertisement about Paraguay where the land is plentiful. "You just have to scatter the seeds and they will grow," says the article. Carolus gets a bag of money from his father and gets on a boat. A priest who will help him find some land is waiting for him at the port of Asunción. Carolus hands over his bag of money, but the priest disappears a day later. He barely speaks a word of Spanish but understands that there are some Belgians living in southern Paraguay and that there could be some land available. The whole area is full of foreigners—especially Germans, but also many Japanese, Russians, Ukrainians, Poles, and Belgians. After World War II, many Nazi sympathizers fled to Paraguay. Carolus wants nothing to do with that; he has come for farming and to find a girl. "If you don't find a girl within three years, you can come back home," Carolus' parents whispered to their son.

A priest takes him to a boarding school church where a dozen ladies are sitting around patiently. "Have your pick," says the priest. Carolus takes a good look at the ladies, but one of them has a limp, another one is a bit sick in the head, and they all are suffering from some ailment.

A little while later, he is given food in the canteen. There he meets Erica who cooks and serves the food. They end up getting married and have 15 children. "Fifteen? That's a big family," Zoë says to Erica.

Yesterday afternoon we stopped in Carolus' small village and asked if Belgians still live there. That's how we find ourselves sitting around a kitchen table chatting with a Belgian family.

"That's how it used to be. We are a blessed family," she continues in a Flemish-German dialect. My husband passed away, but all the children are healthy.

That same evening, we sit at her daughter's table and eat Belgian fries with real mayonnaise. After the kilos of *chipas,* the Paraguayan corn cookies, and the spoiled croquette, nothing tastes as good as a typical Belgian dinner.

Suffering in El Chaco

As we cycle further north, the words "El Chaco" are enough to make us shiver. The Chaco is a semiarid desert that covers more than half of Paraguay, but less than 10 percent of the population lives there. It is "life-threatening" and "there is absolutely nothing," everyone tells us with wide eyes. At the same time, there are more inspiring stories about unspoiled nature and rare animals such as anteaters, tapirs, and pumas. Maybe we are stubborn, naive, or just curious, because we set off on our bikes toward the "green hell," as prepared as we can be.

With 10 kilos of food, 30 bananas, and two large 5-liter bottles of water, we start Ruta 9, better known as the Transchaco. 800 kilometers (500 miles) on a dead straight road, as flat as a pancake. Along the first of those kilometers, we are harassed by traffic, but the further we disappear into the depths of the desert, the more isolated and warmer it gets. Soon we encounter the dangers of the Chaco: unbearable heat, millions of mosquitoes, and demoralizing desperation. It is 100 percent suffering and 0 percent enjoyment. The heat is so oppressive we can barely stand it. We want to pedal harder to catch a breeze, but pedaling harder only makes us sweat more. We drink liters of water, but our thirst is unquenchable. Yearning for shade, we look for a moment of rest, but the Chaco knows no rest. Soon our eyes become heavy trying to avoid the reality of the mile markers. "121, 122. Oh, I'm going insane," Zoë says, "I have to do something."

For miles and miles, we try to forget the suffering—our aching butts, our thirst, and the heat—with games from our childhood. "I see, I see what you don't see and it's green," says Olivier. "The whole Chaco is green, Olivier!"

As far as the eye can see there is nothing but high grass where mosquitoes breed, and poisonous snakes lurk. We have only been on the road for three days, but we are already worn out. At night we don't sleep because our winter tent is hotter than a sauna. During the day, we are on the run from the heat and mosquitoes. We've changed our schedule. At 5:30 a.m., we are on our bikes, and by 11 a.m., we have already cycled more than 100 kilometers (62 miles). The rest of the day, we hide in the shade or in a small room with all the doors and windows closed to escape the mosquitoes.

Over the course of our journey, there have been many moments of suffering—some fleeting, some lasting days. But most of the time, we enjoy it. Or rather, we enjoy mentally overcoming the physical elements. It gives us strength. In reality, mental challenges are always tougher than physical ones. We have withstood hundreds of pains like blisters, abrasions, muscle aches, cramps, and bruises. We have dealt with bad weather, washboard roads, dead ends, flat tires, cold, wet shoes, smelly socks, and thousands of insects. We have endured ants that eat our food, angry horseflies, black flies, and bloodthirsty mosquitoes. Although overcoming such hardships can be extremely satisfying, sometimes our motivation just runs out.

Willpower

"I can't do it anymore," says Zoë as we sit on the road, exhausted after a week in El Chaco.

"Do you want to stop?" Olivier asks.

"No, of course, I don't want to stop," Zoë replies fiercely. "I know that it'll be worth it all in the end. We still have to see that puma." The thought of seeing such a majestic wild beast keeps us moving onward.

It's the morning of day nine and we stand next to our bikes, amazed. It has been raining and the streets have turned into one huge mud puddle. Zoë has her jacket on and is shivering a little from the cold. The sun is hiding behind the clouds, and the wind is coming from the opposite direction. It is 20 degrees cooler, and the mosquitoes have disappeared. "Wonderful!" shouts Olivier. "We have two fewer enemies today." Finally, we are enjoying cycling again, and our mind games are no longer necessary.

Suddenly, Olivier whispers with urgency. "Look!" A big, brown, beautiful cat crosses right in front of us. It's a puma! It calmly crosses the road, slinking along, apparently oblivious to our presence. Eventually, it disappears into the brush.

We are both pumped full of adrenaline. For the next 20 kilometers (12.4 miles), we forget all about the pain. "Never give up, there's always a reward," Zoë says proudly. "But what a sacrifice to see a puma." "It was totally worth the suffering," Olivier concludes. "We're going to make it; in a few days we'll be in Bolivia!" and he grabs Zoë's hand. "Well done, darling."

Hidden Secrets

Discovering New Customs and Culture in Bolivia

We survived the Chaco and proudly crossed the border into Bolivia. We always look forward to a new country. It is an opportunity to make comparisons and discover new things. In colorful letters, *Bolivia te espera* is written on the border post. Bolivia is waiting for you. "We're waiting for you too!" Zoë shouts back. Our senses are ready to discover the secrets of this new country.

The border post lies in complete desolation. Yearningly, we look forward to the first village. Only then do we learn the great differences. When we arrive, we don't know where to start. Our hands can hardly keep up with our thoughts as we jot down our observations in our notebook. What is distinctive about this culture, and what are its hidden secrets? Walking down the street we see *cholitas;* women with bowler hats, long skirts, and woolen socks as well as Mennonites—blond-haired white men in blue overalls who live a traditional lifestyle like the Amish. Olivier's legs quicken when we reach the market. There are new treats to try everywhere. We feel like kids in a candy shop. We ask about everything. What is this? What is that? How is it made? Where does it come from? What is it called?

Soon we see the differences. "Oh, that's cheaper than in Paraguay," or "that looks like a Bolivian specialty." We are looking for bread but only see signs that say *pollo frito, picante de pollo, milaneza de pollo,* and *pollo al spiedo.* Apparently, they only serve chicken. "Don't they eat anything else here?" Zoë asks. We eat dozens of snacks and try strange beverages. Then it's time for serious things. We look for a bank to get bolivianos, we buy a SIM card with data, and we learn what groceries are available for our meals.

It's hot in the Bolivian Chaco, but not like the draining heat in the green hell of Paraguay. There are no mosquitoes either. We enjoy winding roads, beautiful green mountain landscapes, and lots of life. We cycle through an orchestra of singing birds. Green, blue, and red parrots screech as we cycle by, and toucans fly with us from tree to tree. Our energy level doubles every day.

"Do you think we can sleep in a fire department tonight? Or pitch our tent in a yard?" Zoë asks. We don't need to worry too much. Our budget allows us to sleep in hotels every night. "I do miss our encounters with local people," Zoë says as we cycle along a beautiful tarmac road. "I guess that's a disadvantage of being able to afford everything. Because we don't have to be creative in our search for food or places to sleep, we miss out on meeting people."

At the end of the afternoon, we cycle into a small village, but nobody has a yard. Dazed, we sit on the central square and think about how we'll cope. A curious man comes up with the answer. He is eager to practice his English and sits next to us on the bench. He invites us to his hostel and offers us a free room.

"What do you usually have for breakfast," Zoë asks after a while. "Bread," he says deadpan. "Where do you buy it?" "Look for a white cloth over a stick," he says, "everyone who sells bread hangs a white cloth outside when they have fresh bread."

"Aha, a secret discovery!" Although we learn a lot about the culture from walking the streets, like in other countries, we discover the real soul of the country by sitting around the kitchen tables with locals.

A lost baby goat

We are taking photos when Zoë spots a weakened baby goat. She picks it up and sees that it can barely stand and is severely malnourished.

"What do we do? There's no one around here." She doesn't want to leave the poor animal to die, so she takes matters into her own hands. She wraps the kid in a shopping bag and gets back on her bike. With the goat in her arms, we cycle until we reach a farm. The farmer and his wife look at us with mouths agape when they see Zoë with the kid. She asks if they are goat herders, and they nod their heads.

"Good," says Zoë, "Can you raise this goat then? It needs milk." Zoë is already handing them the kid before they have answered the question. We are pragmatic enough to realize that the poor little goat might end up on the menu that night, but even that would be better than leaving it to slowly die by the roadside.

As we cross the border from Paraguay to Bolivia, tropical life returns. Nature is beautifully green, toucans and parrots fly above our heads, and waterfalls resound in the distance (above). Leaving tropical Santa Cruz, the landscape becomes drier again and cacti return (opposite).

A train descends from 4,000 meters (13,000 feet) to the city of Potosí. A loud horn sounds at every turn. There are no barriers, traffic lights, or warning signals. One evening, we have to walk a few hundred meters on the railroad tracks with our bikes to get to a camping spot.

The specter of illness

For the third month in a row, Zoë's periods have been irregular. She passes black menstrual blood at odd times. When we arrive in Santa Cruz, Zoë looks up the possible causes of her symptoms. A long list of possibilities emerges from malignant to inconsequential.

We are staying with Olivier's family friend, Nair. She tries to help us find a good gynecologist, but it's not that easy. The healthcare system in Bolivia consists of private and public hospitals with many doctors having individual practices. In addition, we have travel insurance and without notifying them, we are not allowed to do anything. We feel extremely healthy, never use medication, and except for seasickness and food poisoning, have not been ill. Nair is also confident that we are healthy, although she does think that there is far too little fat on our bodies. She says that we cannot leave before Olivier has gained 5 kilos and Zoë has the results from the gynecologist.

When we enter the hospital, we have to pay cash at the counter before we can see a doctor. The money disappears into a cardboard box. We wait for hours and hours, only to be told that the doctor will not be coming today. We have to come back the next day and wait again.

Finally, Zoë's name is called. She will need three different examinations. At the first, a woman who is dressed like a cleaner asks Zoë to take off her hospital gown. "I'll wait for the doctor," Zoë says patiently. "She's late, so I'll do this for her," is the reply.

In the second room, there is a man with a mustache and a freshly stubbed-out cigarette sitting at his desk reading the paper. He doesn't look up, doesn't introduce himself, and tells her to take a seat. He then rolls his desk chair over and positions himself between Zoë's legs. Before he begins, he coughs vigorously and a rush of air wafts between her legs. A feeling of unease overwhelms her. "Come on, Zoë, don't be silly," she tells herself sternly.

A little later we get the results. "You have several cysts on your ovaries and an infection," the doctor explains. When Zoë asks where the cysts and inflammation have come from, the answer is, "You know, it's late, I want to go home. Tomorrow, I have more time."

We leave Santa Cruz with a round of antibiotics, and a recommendation for Zoë to have another check-up in three months. We decide to cycle on but will soon learn that we can feel perfectly healthy with a lot of mystery inside our bodies.

A herd of alpacas roams the barren and inhospitable highlands of western Bolivia. Alpacas are kept in herds and are bred specifically for their fleece, which is used to make knitted and woven items.

Another planet?

"Shall we find a place here and have a rest day?" suggests Olivier. There is only one hostel in the village, so we don't really have a choice.

"*Dinamarca!*" the daughter shouts proudly when she sees the little flag on Olivier's bike and thinks we are from Denmark. "*Bélgica,*" Olivier says. A moment later, the family stands around our unfolded world map. We explain our route, while the family is still searching for Bolivia on the map. "What's that big blue country?" the father asks. "That's the ocean, Daddy!" his daughter says quickly.

Almost every day we tell our story, but in the mountains of Bolivia, conversations are limited to everything people know from their immediate surroundings. "How many cows do you have?" the mother asks Zoë. "None. There are just a few farmers, but they have a lot of cattle. The rest of us live in cities and work with computers," she explains. They can't imagine it.

"What a cultural difference," says Zoë. "It feels like we're from another planet." Cultures are like planets. They are separate worlds that have their own attractive force. Gravitational pull is the norm, and values are derived from centuries of traditions and customs. It is extremely interesting to study other planets, but as outsiders, we speak a different language. We judge a culture based on our own planet and way of thinking. In Bolivia, we learn this for the first time, but also in Canada, we learn to understand why people eat seal, while we donate money to campaigns against hunting in the Netherlands. We learn why shooting bears is legal, even though we think it is pathetic. We learn why someone is a Trump supporter or why in one country it is rude to leave after one night and in another country, it is rude to stay longer. We learn that every country and every person has their own perspective and frame of reference. If we want to understand those perspectives, we must look through their lenses of thinking, upbringing, and environment.

After the rest day, we climb higher into the Andes. We follow an old route with many unpaved roads and steep climbs. The antibiotics in Zoë's body have had quite an effect. With stomach cramps and weak legs, she plows her way up through the loose sand. Trucks cover us in thick layers of dust and belch out plumes of black smoke. We find a small restaurant for lunch and plop down on the chairs. Our tablemates are surprised to see two Westerners, especially when they hear about our trip. "*Pura bici?*" one man asks with open eyes. All by bicycle? No one cycles here; cycling is not part of the culture. Someone who cycles cannot afford a motorcycle and is by definition poor. The fact that we cycle around the world for fun is incomprehensible to them. But is the person behind the different language, customs, and hand gestures really so different?

"Can I pay your meal?" the man asks. "My contribution to your adventure." At its roots, people are much more alike than different. In the universe of cultures, the sun's gravitation pull is a unifying factor, but so are basic human desires and dignity. Everyone wants a roof over their head, friends, and happiness. Everyone wants to do well in life, and we see that every day—no matter what planet we are cycling on.

Small stores in Sucre sell a wide variety of medicinal remedies, from special herbs to llama fetuses (opposite). Bowler hats are a main part of traditional dress among *cholitas*, the Bolivian women in the Andes (left). A traditional festival in the small village of Huachacalla. There are long parades with hours of music and dancing (above).

High in the Andes, the climate is extremely harsh. Only llamas and a rare generation of resilient people are capable of surviving at such high altitudes. We are only passing through. We camp at an altitude of 3,500 meters (11,500 feet) on the way to Uyuni (below).

On the border of Bolivia and Peru, north of La Paz, lies Lake Titicaca, the largest lake in South America and often called the highest navigable lake in the world.

Old jeep tracks and the contours of mountains are the only guidelines on the salt flats.
The mountains never seem to get closer, and it is impossible to estimate the distance.

Cycling in heaven

It takes us two weeks of lactic acid in our muscles to cycle from tropical Santa Cruz to heaven. Salar de Uyuni is located at 3,650 meters (11,975 feet) above sea level. The plain is a giant prehistoric lake that has dried up and transformed into a huge salt flat. Millions of salt crystals form a beautiful pattern of hexagonal tiles.

With wide eyes, we scan the plain before us. "Where do we go?" Zoë asks. A few mountains can be seen on the horizon, but otherwise, it's impossible to get our bearings. We are looking for an island in the middle of the salt flats with a restaurant to refill our water, about 70 kilometers (43 miles) away. It is impossible to pick it out from here. There are no official roads and no signposts, only jeep tracks. Zoë aligns her compass and sets a course for the northwest.

Olivier quickly picks up a stone and straps it under his rear rack. "Why are you taking a stone?" Zoë asks. "To knock the tent pegs into the salt," he says. "Smart!" she says with a smile.

We disappear like dots on the horizon and are swallowed up by the big white sky. The hexagonal tiles are sometimes perfectly flat and sometimes bumpier than a cobblestone road. Occasionally we see small black flecks on the horizon that move agonizingly slow. They are tourist jeeps taking day tours. They don't see us; we are much too small. At night we camp in the middle of the salt flats. Beforehand, we feared that a jeep would drive over our tent at night. Now we know that the chances of that are minuscule. The temperature cools to -12°C (10°F). We shiver from the cold until the first rays of sunlight warm the tent. We ponder that maybe there's another cyclist 100 kilometers (62 miles) away, sleeping on the same salt flat, just as anonymous as we are. For four days we disappear into heaven. We don't meet anyone. We are so anonymous and so alone that we could cycle naked.

FAQs on the road

After the two opening questions, "where do you come from?" and "where are you going?" a third question always followed.

Slowly, we noticed that the third question or comment typified the culture and thinking patterns of the country we were in.

When we told people in Bolivia that we are from Holanda and Bélgica, they thought deeply. "Is that in La Paz?" they then asked, certain that Holanda and Bélgica were villages in one of Bolivia's provinces. They couldn't imagine traveling by bike from another country.

Many questions were about our daily lives on our bikes. Where do we sleep? Do we cycle all night? How much do the bikes weigh? What do we do when it rains?

Even in Sweden or Norway people asked, "Are you from France and Germany?" when they saw our flags. Perhaps it wasn't so strange that a Bolivian farmer didn't know Bélgica.

The salt flats are a 10,000-square-kilometer (3,850-square-mile) perfectly flat camping spot (above). Life is almost impossible here, but flamingos, vicuñas, and domesticated llamas are able to survive in these harsh conditions (opposite).

We cycle all the way from Uyuni to Sabaya on the northern end of Salar de Coipasa, a smaller salt flat north of Salar de Uyuni. It takes us five days to cross both salt flats, almost 300 kilometers (185 miles) on a salty surface. Afterward, we have to clean the bicycles to remove all the salt.

Footsteps of the Incas

Time Traveling through Peru

Ellen, Zoë's mother, is going to visit us in Peru. "I'll just follow like a mother goose follows the little ones," she says as we make initial plans by phone.

"Mom, you know how we travel, right? We sleep in the cheapest places with saggy beds where there is sand, mold, and hair in the bathtub," Zoë replies cautiously. With Ellen's words, "a bed is just a bed, after all," the trip is planned. Zoë's mother flies alone to Cuzco to travel around with us for two weeks.

Ellen hasn't seen us for a year. She hears our fluent Spanish and sees how we move around the country almost like locals. We leave the bikes for two weeks and preplan our route, but everything else we decide on the spur of the moment. Every morning we move to a new place. After a bumpy ride in a crammed minivan, we start looking for a *hospedaje,* or hostel. Normally, we go for the cheapest option available. The first night in Peru—two weeks ago—cost us barely 10 soles, two and a half euros.

With Ellen, we have to be a little more flexible, but we don't want to pay more than 20 soles. We walk from door to door, ask the price, check the rooms, and compare different places.

"I thought I was the frugal Dutchman," Ellen says when we still don't approve of the fourth hotel. The highlight is lunch. We eat for five soles, about 20 cents in euros. Six soles, about 25 cents, we think is too much. We laugh about it to ourselves, but still, we don't stop to think about the real value of one sol. For a normal tourist, six soles is ridiculously cheap, but to us, it is 20 percent more expensive than our norm.

"If we can get something for 25 euros, we wouldn't want to pay 30 euros for the same thing, would we?" we try to explain.

"Dear dears, you really are too stingy," says Ellen. She is unfortunately right, and we later enjoy a restaurant where we pay seven soles. Afterward, we feel a little ashamed of our uncompromising frugality.

Two fishing boats on the Peruvian side of Lake Titicaca (opposite). Slow travel is the secret to discovering real local culture. In an old football stadium, schoolchildren gather to perform traditional dances for their parents (above).

Historic Cuzco is a great place for traveling back in time to the Inca Empire. The Incas cleverly built terraces based on the sun, moon, and water. Many structures are still a mystery to historians (above). A woman performs a traditional dance during Inti Raymi, the festival of the sun (opposite, top).

Tourist attractions are often too much of a detour on a bicycle, but the Inca citadel of Machu Picchu is well worth the effort.
At 6 a.m., we hike all the way to the top to admire the sunrise.

At the ancient Maras Salt Mines, salt is still extracted by evaporating the intensely salty water that comes from an underground stream.
The stream is routed through an intricate system of small channels so that the water flows gradually to the hundreds of terraced ponds.

The ring-shaped ruins of Moray were believed to serve as a site of agricultural experimentation for the Incas. From top to bottom, the terraces have a 5 °C (9 °F) temperature range. With the way the terraces are situated, the sunlight hits the terraces at different angles and intensities.

We make camp at an altitude of 4,256 meters (13,963 feet) at the foot of Laguna Arhuaycocha in the Cordillera Blanca mountains. The whole mountain range is part of the Huascarán National Park, a paradise for hikers and climbers.

The mountainside of Peru

After two weeks of vacation with Ellen, we leave Cuzco heading north. We follow the ridge of the Andes and immediately face a 60-kilometer (37-mile) climb. It is not the easiest way, but in our minds, we have bought two tickets for an imaginary play—*The Mountainside of Peru*. We are looking forward to the drama that unfolds. We reset our minds to zero and plop down on our saddles again. Let the play begin.

Down in the valley, a tropical climate prevails with palm trees and banana plantations. Old ladies with big smiles and shiny gold teeth wave at us. They trudge up the mountain carrying large bales of sugar cane. It seems as if their bony knees will buckle at any moment. Babies' heads dangle out uncomfortably from colorful wrapped clothes on the back of young women.

Gradually we climb higher, and the tropical humidity changes to thinner mountain air. We cycle past adobe houses with wooden balconies whose walls are painted with the names of mayoral candidates. Each candidate has his own logo, one a soccer ball, another a drop of water, or a shovel. The clothes on the clothesline tell which houses are inhabited, and there are sometimes other signs of life even in the most dilapidated houses. We see old women separating sand from grain, doing laundry, or weaving intricate cloths in front of their humble homes. Sometimes we can peek inside and see large mounds of corn and potatoes filling the whole room. The magnificent snowcapped peaks of the Andes are the backdrop to these scenes.

The way to the top is tough, but the road is filled with people cheering us on. Little children with blushed cheeks and dark eyes stare at us and shout, "*Mami, mami, gringos!*" and hide behind open doors. They always call us *gringos,* or *gringa* if they are addressing Zoë alone. "*Gringa, no tienes fría?*" Aren't you cold, asks an old woman by the side of the road when Zoë rides by in short sleeves and shorts.

Above 3,000 meters (10,000 feet), we see canvas tents which function as restaurants. Inside a worker simmers pork and potatoes in a pan over an open fire for hungry truckers or other travelers who might pass through. A simple table and four plastic garden chairs complete the restaurant. Mountain water flows down the wide ditches beside the road. Cars stop in the middle of the road while people leisurely wash their cars. Further on, large bags of potatoes lie in the ditches waiting to be rinsed clean. People even wash mattresses there, kicking out the dirt as they rinse. Between the houses chickens and cows run, while pigs regularly cross the street, often followed by old women in bowler hats carrying wooden sticks and hissing at them.

"Isn't this special?" Zoë says as she discusses everything in detail. Olivier, needing all of his oxygen, simply nods.

As the valley recedes below us in the distance, we realize how high we have climbed. For the last few meters, well above 4,000 meters (13,000 feet), we find ourselves enveloped in clouds. We cross the mountain pass and begin a 60-kilometer (37-mile) descent to end back among the palm trees and banana plantations.

The cracked rim

On the long descent to Huánuco, Olivier felt something ticking as he braked. There was a crack in his bike's rim. Day after day, he walks past all the bike shops in town looking for a replacement but to no avail. They only sell kid's bikes and small mountain bikes. He searches the internet and calls bicycle stores, but our rim size doesn't seem to exist here.

"Pedro lives in Lima, maybe he can help?" Zoë suggests. On the plane from Amsterdam to Lima, Zoë's mother sat next to Pedro and Yago. Pedro was sold when Ellen told our story, and he spontaneously invited us to Lima and his brother's hotel on the coast. We give him a call. "Lima is our last chance," we explain. Pedro isn't surprised. "Where is that store—I will go there immediately?" is his reply. An hour later, he sends a picture via WhatsApp with the correct rim in hand. "I'll send the rim on the night bus," Pedro assures us. In Peru, it's quite normal for long-distance buses to work as parcel services. "And it is all paid, my contribution to your adventure," Pedro adds quickly, "now you can come to my brother's hotel by bicycle."

After two years, our bags, racks, and fenders are covered in blue duct tape and held together by zip ties. They are indispensable equipment in our travels, and we are constantly repairing them. We sew our clothes, shoes, and sleeping bags and put new zippers on the tent. Only when something is beyond repair do we throw it away. We also try to do our own bicycle maintenance and repairs whenever possible.

The view from Punta Union, halfway along the Santa Cruz trail in Huascarán National Park (opposite, bottom). Climbs of 50–60 kilometers (30–40 miles) are no exception in Peru. In the south, the gradients are pleasant, but farther north, it gets steep (above).

Olivier walks to the bicycle store, holding the old wheel in his left hand and the brand-new rim in his right.

"How much will you charge to build my wheel?"

The bike mechanic has to do the math and is unsure what to say. "100 soles," he finally offers. One euro and thirty cents to build a new wheel? The man will have to work for at least an hour and a half. Olivier pays him 300 soles. In the Netherlands, we would pay at least 80 euros, and even that price would have been worth it to continue our journey.

Known in the unknown

North of Huaraz the landscape changes. The gradual, long climbs become steeper and more direct. The route becomes rough and more unpaved. There are hardly any cars on the roads. We can climb and suffer undisturbed.

"We have to recommend this route to other cyclists. I think this road is still unknown," Olivier says after we have descended 2,000 meters (6,500 feet) of altitude in one go. During the descent, we can see our destiny—countless switchbacks snake up on the other side. Suddenly two cyclists appear, waving at us. "*Hola Zoë, hola Olivier!*" the woman shouts.

We stare at them our mouths agape. "We've been following you on Instagram for a long time and are so happy to meet you." The Taiwanese couple is cycling from Colombia to Ushuaia. Are we becoming famous?

Crossing an old suspension bridge along the Mantaro River in central Peru (opposite, bottom). The highest point we reach by bicycle in Peru is 4,878 meters (16,004 feet) above sea level (top).

On our way to Huaraz, we feel very small next to the majestic peaks in the Cordillera Blanca.
At these altitudes, we need to wear gloves and warm clothes on our bicycles.

Along the Santa River, the roads are fairly flat, but there always comes a time when we have to cross the mountains.
We welcome the challenge of cycling at high altitudes.

In northern Peru, horses are still used to separate the wheat from the chaff (above). Between the months of July and October, the northern coast of Peru serves as a breeding ground for humpback whales (opposite).

Arguments and apologies

We make our last descent from the Andes and set course for the coast where we will stay for a few days at Pedro's brother's hotel. The cool mountain air gives way to burning sun. Switchbacks are swapped for straight roads through desert-like landscapes. The mosquitoes return and our sleeping bags become superfluous.

We had imagined a route with white beaches and palm trees, but in reality, we cycle through a monotonous land of pumpjacks, sandstorms, and withered bushes. We take out our frustrations on each other. Arguing away, we cycle against the wind.

A man with a donkey rides up to us. He is sitting on a cart loaded with small branches. Every day he drives three hours through the sandstorms looking for firewood. We argue because we have to cross the desert for a few days on our way to a luxury hotel. For him, this is a daily way of life. Ashamed, we apologize to each other.

Right after the town of Pallasca, we have to cross a river to get to the other side of the valley. Dozens of hairpin curves down and countless up. We end the day with 2,400 meters (7,875 feet) of elevation gain and a good night's sleep.

Strange Encounters

The Ups and Downs of Cycling through Ecuador

After four days of rest on the beach, we cruise to the border of Ecuador with a glorious tailwind. In the distance, two cyclists are riding in the opposite direction, fighting against the strong wind. We stop for a chat. They are two Colombian cyclists on their way to Santiago, Chile. They tell us they are going to cycle 130 kilometers (81 miles) today.

"You have beautiful panniers," Zoë says in admiration.

They proudly tell us the panniers are homemade and let us peek inside. Olivier takes a quick photo because the two are in a hurry.

"Those two are crazy, cycling against the wind for those distances each day," Olivier says.

Right across the border the landscape changes yet again. The coast of Ecuador is where our Chiquita bananas come from. We cycle 80 kilometers (50 miles) through a banana jungle in the heart of the industry. We regularly have to wait when sturdy workmen pull about 20 bunches along the road. A steel rail often runs from the plantation to the factory. In the first village after the plantations, we knock on the door of the fire department for a place to sleep. The commander is shocked and says, "Have you cycled through that area? It's full of drug cartels; it is extremely dangerous."

Two weeks later, we post our photo of the handmade panniers on Instagram. We immediately receive comments from other cyclists, and we click on a link someone sends us. It's a video of Chilean customs removing two bikes from the cargo area of a bus. They cut open the bottom of the instantly recognizable panniers and discover black packages. The pair we had met were smuggling 18 kilograms (40 pounds) of marijuana in the double bottoms of their handmade panniers. They traveled almost entirely by bus. They only cycled stretches with police checks, such as border crossings. We laugh about our strange encounter but also feel sad that they are damaging the image of world cyclists and worry it might make border crossings harder for others in the future.

When we get to the hills of Ecuador, we have two very memorable nights. The first evening, we find an abandoned police station by the side of the road which seems like the ideal

Espeletia trees thrive in La Reserva ecológica el Ángel in northern Ecuador. The trees are nicknamed "big monks" (opposite). The Cotopaxi is among the highest active volcanoes in the world and the second-highest summit in Ecuador. The last eruption was between August 2015 and January 2016 (above).

place to spend the night. We are sheltered from the strong wind and the missing window creates an open-air cinema effect. With a twinkling starry sky in view, we fall asleep. In our dreams, we are bumping along a bad road. Or is it a truck passing too close? Confused, Zoë suddenly sits upright on her sleeping mat. With two hands she slaps Olivier's back. "An earthquake!" she shouts happily.

Olivier wakes up with a jolt. The realization that a half-collapsed building is perhaps not the safest shelter in an earthquake snaps us out of our joy. We run out of the house just as the seismic tremors pass.

Still talking about the earthquake from the previous night, we get permission to sleep in a *choza,* a typical shepherd's hut in the highlands of Ecuador. Three children step in as we are creating our home one evening. Fascinated, they watch us roll out our sleeping mats and set up our stove. They take turns plopping down on our mats and cuddling in our down sleeping bags. When one of them asks what time it is in Belgium, and we tell them that our parents are already asleep, they look wide-eyed.

"How does that work?"

So, we explain how the earth rotates around its axis and that our days are much shorter in winter. They are amazed. The children live almost at the equator, so they have about 12 hours of daylight year-round. Later that evening, they bring us hot tea and fried plantains and feast on our pasta.

We avoid the main road because of heavy traffic, but the alternatives are single-track trails and cobblestone streets. Our vintage bicycles are not quite made for this, but they survive (above). The high grassland ecosystem of El Cajas National Park outside of Cuenca, Ecuador (below). A traditional festival in Cotacachi, just north of Quito (opposite, bottom).

Cuenca is a beautiful colonial city with many authentic buildings. It is one of the few bike-friendly cities in South America. Grilled plantains filled with cheese are a typical roadside snack in Ecuador (above).

Unexpected news

We have had a hectic feeling cycling through Ecuador for the past two weeks. The main roads are too busy, but the smaller roads are too steep and full of cobblestones. Not one day have we reached our daily target, and we are barely ticking off 50 kilometers (31 miles) per day. Every day that passes, we feel more and more rushed. There is no time to experience the culture. Olivier's parents are coming to visit us, and we will meet in Cancún, Mexico. A month ago, Olivier said confidently, "With a tight schedule, we will make it without any problems." But little by little, that schedule is slipping.

Almost four months have passed since the hospital visit in Bolivia. Zoë feels healthy and full of confidence as we walk to the hospital in Quito. Everything looks more like the hospitals we're used to back home, leaving her feeling at ease.

"So young and so many problems," the doctor says after a quick look at his monitor.

Zoë immediately glances at Olivier. With a questioning look, she tries to figure out if she has missed something. "What are all these problems?" she asks, confused.

"Your IUD is too low so you can get pregnant, you have polycystic ovaries, and I see a large unknown mass here," the doctor tells her. "We will have to operate on that," and he gestures for Zoë to get dressed again.

We sit in the waiting room, our heads dizzy with questions. "What do you think?" Olivier asks. "I have no idea," Zoë says.

A few minutes later a nurse gives us the results, asking if we would like to sign them. "Can't we talk to the doctor anymore?" Zoë asks. "Everything is explained on paper," says the nurse, but there are barely five lines of medical Spanish. Outside the hospital, tears well up in Zoë's eyes, shocked by the unexpected news and confused by uncertainties.

"Do I need surgery? Why didn't they discover this in Bolivia? I don't understand. Where? Here in Ecuador? I'm not going home!" she cries.

We cycle the Quilotoa Loop with its high peaks along the Quilotoa crater. It is an inactive volcanic crater with a copper-green lake.

We have faith in the hospitals in Ecuador, but everything is different than in the Netherlands. Here the doctor decides, and the patient accepts. We have dozens of questions, but there is no possibility to ask them. Since the first examinations in Bolivia, a colleague of Olivier's mother has been helping us. She is a gynecologist and has worked in Chile for a while. She knows the cultural differences and understands the hospital reports. We send the results immediately and wait for her advice. It is a relief to discuss the medical situation with a familiar voice. She recommends getting another scan in three weeks and having surgery if the diagnosis is confirmed. We decide to continue cycling, although we feel down and full of doubts.

Gratitude and attitudes

While we cycle to northern Ecuador, whole caravans of refugees are walking south. Venezuela is in deep crisis, with hyperinflation and major food shortages. Millions of people are leaving their country and walking to Ecuador or Peru. The situation is so bad that refugees are selling Venezuelan banknotes of 10,000 bolivars for half a euro to tourists. We live on the streets because we want to—they do because they have to. We feel humble and our hearts break as we pass them.

Just before the border of Colombia we leave the main road and cycle inland through the Reservera ecólogica el Ángel. We save the long climb over the cobblestones until the next day and ask for a place to pitch our tent at the first house we see. The man is working outside and calls his wife. She looks concerned. "Where are you from?" she asks and then walks back inside without saying anything. Soon the woman returns, this time with a big smile.

"Come in, are you hungry?" It is the birthday of the eldest son. According to Ecuadorian tradition, *cuy* is on the menu. "Would you like some guinea pig?" the mother asks. She opens the oven and pulls out a grilled guinea pig. The legs and head are still on. Inwardly we say no, but out of politeness, we say yes.

"It tastes like rabbit," Olivier says, and he realizes that eating rabbit might be as strange as eating guinea pig. The mother's concern is gone, and she treats us like her own children. We are allowed to stay the night and even get her son's room. Later that evening, she tells us why she walked back into the house.

"I was afraid you were Venezuelans. When I heard that you were from another country, I asked the advice of the Virgin Mary. I asked her, 'what should I do? Tell me, what should I do?'"

Now she knows that she made the right choice and that Virgin Mary is protecting her. We count ourselves lucky for her trust and hospitality.

Unusual dishes we ate during our trip
· Grilled guinea pig at a birthday party in Ecuador
· Seal steak with a fisherman's family in Canada
· Pig's skin at a barbecue in Bolivia
· Cow's small intestine in Argentina
· Cow's udder and lips in Ecuador

The gauchos of Ecuador are called *chagras*. They wear *sombreros* (hats) and are famous for their exceptional horseman skills and unwavering dedication to their horses (opposite). Coffee beans dry in the sun (top).

Our hurried schedule forces us to avoid detours in Colombia, but the main roads also offer beautiful scenery. The road from the border of Ecuador to Pasto follows the Río Angasmayo.

An Impossible Decision

Leaving Colombia Too Fast

Our family and friends say, "Come home, you can't have surgery in Colombia." For us, that decision isn't so easy. We have been on the road for two years and have traveled across the earth from the Netherlands to Colombia. We feel at home here and don't want to interrupt our line on the map. We have three options: 1. no surgery, but then there is a high risk that the tumor will grow causing other complications; 2. surgery in the Netherlands, but then we have to interrupt our world trip; or 3. surgery in Colombia. It comes down to the uncertainty of language, culture, and medical facilities versus interrupting our trip. An impossible decision. Whichever path we choose, we only see the disadvantages.

In southern Colombia, we meet Frank and Jacinta. They are, like us, a Dutch-Belgian couple traveling by bicycle, but with 30 years more life experience. We are happy to discuss our dilemma with them.

"Home!" they say in unison. "You're not going to risk your health for an emotional goal in your head," Jacinta says. They have been back three times during their trip, and they assure us that it is nice to be back home.

We were trying to make the decision with our hearts instead of our heads. It takes some time before we are able to see that. We look for the advantages of each option. No surgery is the easy solution, but in doing so we walk away from the problem. Choosing Colombia means we don't interrupt our journey, but in return, we face a whole lot of uncertainties. Choosing the Netherlands cuts our line on the map in half, but we see our family and friends, we have a place to recover, we speak the language, we understand the culture, and we feel more confortable with the doctors and medical equipment.

"If I were in your shoes, I would come home and do the surgery in the Netherlands or Belgium," the Belgian doctor says confidently after a long phone conversation. The chance of complications is real and then we'd be stuck in Colombia for several months. It's the final push that we need. We set a course to the airport in Medellín.

El teleférico la Garrucha is a wooden cable car in the town of Jardín, in the heart of the coffee region. La Garrucha was originally installed as a way of transporting people, supplies, and produce between the town center and the agricultural area to the south (above). Papaya trees thrive in Columbia (right).

Police escort

In the times of Pablo Escobar, Medellín was the center of the Colombian drug industry. Today, that center lies further south in Cali. Until a few years ago, a fierce drug war raged.

"As long as Europe and the U.S. keep using, we'll keep producing," Fernando rightly says. He is a retired Colonel and fought many years against the drug cartels. Many cyclists avoid Cali because it is dangerous, and he thinks that is unfair. We have to change that image today. Fernando has a plan.

A police patrol awaits us in the city. Four cops on bicycles, one motorcycle, and two cars are our private escort through the city. Flanked by the officers, accompanied by flashing police lights and a photographer, we ride through the city like kings. It is their way to show that Cali is safe. Surprised, the Colombians stare at us wondering who warranted such an escort. In the city center, a number of journalists are waiting with cameras. "Is Cali dangerous?" they ask.

With our plans set, we relax and start to take in our surroundings as we ride through Columbia. The villages are colorful with yellow, orange, green, and red houses. The market square is full of terraces where old men in matching white hats sip coffee. They all look like versions of Juan Valdez, the fictional icon of the Colombian coffee trade. The side streets are full of coffee beans drying in the sun, and we see green bunches of bananas being loaded on top of buses.

Outside the villages, we cycle through endless coffee plantations. The coffee culture landscape is a UNESCO World Heritage Site. Here, banana plants and coffee plants grow together. The large leaves of the banana trees provide shade that allows the coffee beans to ripen slowly, improving the quality and taste.

Speed limit

We ride through Colombia as fast as we can. "We can only stay one night; we have to get to the hospital in Medellín," we keep telling our hosts.

Every day, people invite us in, offer fruit, and try to lure us in for a glass of fresh juice. We are racing through a country where the speed limit is almost crawling. "Why don't you stay a week and then take the bus? Surely that's much safer if you really need to go to the hospital."

We stubbornly persist with our desire to ride the whole way. Once Medellín is within reach, we relax and slow down a little. We want to enjoy our last week on the bike for a while. We receive an invitation from Lina via Instagram. She—like many Colombians—loves cycling and would like to meet us.

We park the bikes in front of Lina's door, but before we can knock, the neighbor across the street opens his door. He immediately asks if we want to have lunch with him the next day. It typifies Colombians, their hospitality, and their openness. We are glad that we can say "yes" instead of, "unfortunately, we have to move on." The next afternoon we sit at Martin's table.

"What do you eat on the road?" he asks. We tell him that we usually cook pasta, sometimes with tomato sauce and sometimes with sour cream. During the day we eat bananas or an energy bar.

"Then I hope you will like this." There is so much delicious food on the table that even two hungry cyclists can't finish it all.

The next morning, we are ready to leave. The door across the street opens again. Martin has a plastic bag in his hand. "Some food for the road. Everything you mentioned yesterday," he says with a broad smile.

Exactly three weeks after our last hospital visit, we arrive in Medellín. The medical examination confirms a tumor that seals the deal on our trip home. That same evening, we speak with our travel insurance company, and they organize a flight to Amsterdam in two days.

For two years, we have traveled slowly and carefree, but now things are moving at lightning speed. We feel like we barely know Colombia. It feels like an unwritten last page of a book. We pack the bikes in cardboard boxes ready for the flight because we know our journey will continue. We just don't know exactly where or when.

The Colombian coffee region of El Eje Cafetero is famous for growing and producing the majority of Colombian coffee. Like other towns and villages in the region, Buenos Aires, Colombia, is surrounded by coffee plantations.

Managing Risk

Embracing the Unknown

Managing Risk

We have never released a risk analysis on our trip, but we consciously and unconsciously took measures to mitigate unpleasant and dangerous risks while on the road. Often these were the same measures we would have taken at home.

Here are some examples of risky situations and how we dealt with them:

Rare–negligible
The small annoying things in life that we just accepted.
• A broken fender
• A wasp sting

Very likely–negligible
Small risks are usually minor but are likely to occur. We took measures to reduce their likelihood.
• Travelers' diarrhea: we were careful with what we ate, asked if the water was drinkable, and filtered our water.
• Punctures: we used better quality tires.
• Mosquito bites: we bathed after sports, wore long clothing, and applied insect repellent.

How people viewed us as travelers?

Mostly, people looked at us with great admiration. Yet some people stereotyped us along the way and thought poor cyclists. In some countries, traveling by bicycle represented poverty. Sometimes people just helped us out of pity. But occasionally, people saw us as vagrants and deliberately avoided eye contact.

While in other countries, eyes started to shine at the sight of our two bikes. "How much did they cost?" a curious bystander asked. "Can I have them?" said another boldly.

As far as varying attitudes, the sailboat trip took the crown. During our few weeks in Africa, we were like a floating piece of gold: vacationers. In the eyes of many, we were on a long vacation. We didn't agree. The world trip was our life, our job, and not a "stop" or "break." Writing blogs, editing videos, finding sponsors, and giving presentations consumed almost all of our "free" time. There were also people who thought that we took advantage of the hospitality and help that people offered. Ultimately, we realize that we have no control over how other people view us—positively or negatively. We can only be ourselves.

Most frequently asked questions

• Argentina: "How do our fellow countrymen treat you?"
• Bolivia, Peru, Mexico, and Southern U.S.: "Do you believe in God?" and they sent us on our way with *"que dios les bendiga, cuida y protege"*—may God bless you, guide you, and protect you—or held our hands and prayed aloud.
• Brazil: "Are you married?" and "where are your children?" Eight years as a couple; something must be wrong.
• Colombia: "How long are you staying?" One night was always the wrong answer.
• Peru and Bolivia: "Why don't you go by motorcycle?"
• U.S., Canada, and Europe: "How do you fund your trip?"

Rare–severe
Unexpected but the consequences are severe. We took out travel insurance which covered theft, fire, accidents, and illnesses.
The tumor on Zoë's ovary fell into this category, and our insurance covered it.

Very likely–severe
Our first job was to reduce the possibility of these risks happening at all by trying to avoid the danger.
• Dangerous traffic situations: we avoided busy roads, never cycled in the dark, wore helmets, and had mirrors, lights, and bells on our bikes.
• Bicycles stolen (fortunately, this never happened): we always locked our bicycles, never left valuable things on them, took the bikes inside our hotel rooms, and never left them unattended at grocery stores.

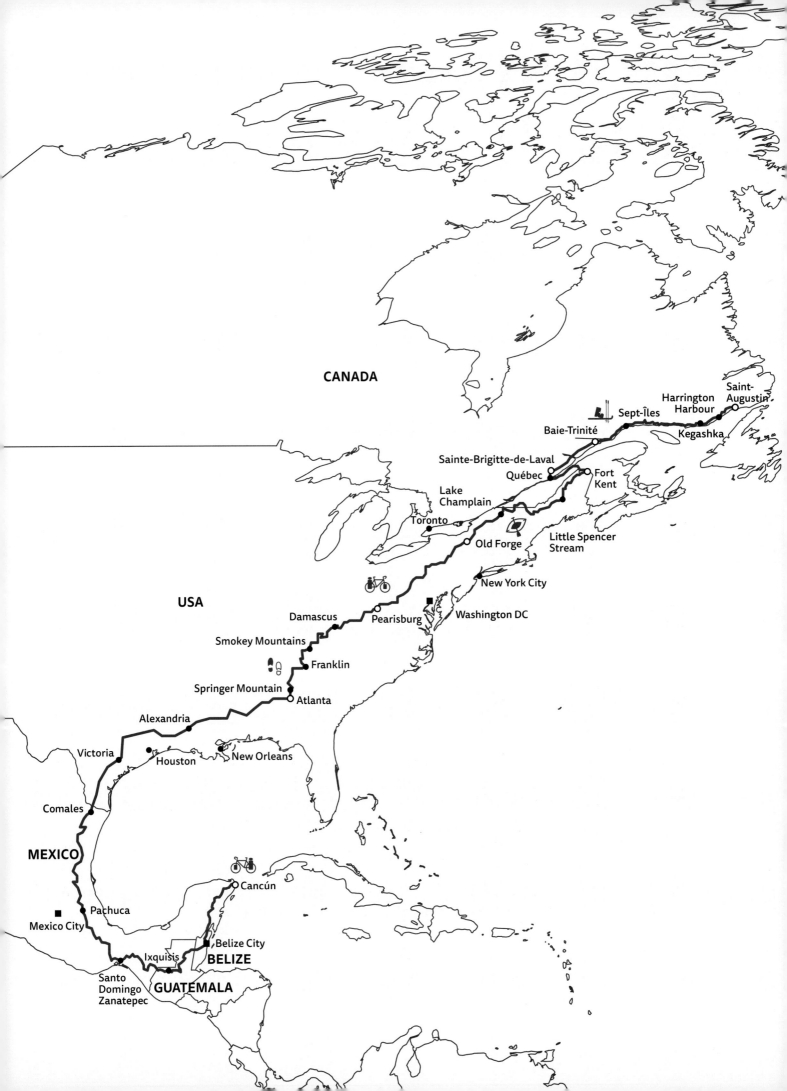

CROSSING NORTH AMERICA

Traveling by Human Power from Mexico to Canada

"And for you, sir?" the flight attendant asks in Dutch. Olivier is startled by the Dutch voice, but he already knows what he wants. "A glass of milk, please." The flight attendant pours a cup full and hands him a *stroopwafel* with it. Olivier looks out the window. Everything is so familiar, yet new.

"Look at all those rectangular fields," Zoë points out, "The Netherlands is so structured. And so flat."

"Welcome home," the flight attendant says as we touch down on Dutch soil with a soft thud. Zoë takes Olivier's hand and sighs deeply.

"It's not that I'm *not* happy, but it's not that I'm very happy either," she tries to sort out her confused feelings. "It's still our journey, nothing is broken or pulled apart. We're still not at our end destination. It's just a stop in our crazy adventure," Olivier tries to perk Zoë up.

The Yucatán Peninsula is the center of ancient Mayan civilization. The region is still home to the Mayans, one of the largest Indigenous populations in North America. Cycling through the villages, the culture is still visible in the houses, clothes, and language.

Home and Abroad

Restarting our journey

We get into our familiar car, but our senses are keen like we are in a new country. We are reminded of everything that we had forgotten about our home. "Look at all those cyclists. And they all have panniers, they look like travelers," Zoë says cheerfully. There are Dutch voices on the radio, billboards are written in large Dutch letters along the road, and all the license plates are yellow and black. Zoë feels elated and happy. Olivier feels nothing in particular, but says contentedly, "It feels like home."

Two days later, all the sense of newness is nearly gone. It feels normal again to flush toilet paper, have hot showers, and enjoy freshly squeezed juice every morning. We enjoy being home and the luxury is quickly replacing our basic life of the past two years. We almost forget why we are here.

Zoë finds it terrifying that a surgeon is going to just cut into her body. She is afraid that the surgery will cause some permanent injury and that she won't be able to do everything anymore. Further examinations have shown that the tumor is benign. Zoë will have laparoscopic surgery, which is a routine procedure, but that doesn't put her at ease. She reports to the hospital on the day of the surgery scared to death.

Zoë's surgery is successful, and she rests afterward. After four weeks, she begins with abdominal exercises. The small lump she feels during the exercises worries her. At her final checkup, she tells the gynecologist who is immediately concerned. "It's probably a hernia," says the doctor, "A small hernia normally will not worsen, but since you're going to be so active, I think we should resolve it."

For the second time, Zoë goes under the knife. This time she is not as frightened, but she is upset and frustrated that they are messing with her muscles again and that we will have to wait six additional weeks to continue our trip.

The preparations for the next part of our journey have been ready for a long time. We can't wait to start our new plan on human power through North America: 7,000 kilometers (4,350 miles) by bicycle, 1,000 kilometers (620 miles) of hiking, and 1,200 kilometers (745 miles) by canoe.

A ticking bomb

Our restart begins in Mexico. One flight and we are back on our adventure. We put the panniers on our bikes, and we pick up where we left off. We're looking forward to our new plans, but when we start riding in Cancún, we are reminded that life on the road isn't always so simple. We struggle to find our familiar rhythm. Our journey has taken on a new dimension with new goals. Somehow this has left us conflicted. The panniers filled with new gear don't feel like us.

From Cancún, we cycle into the jungle. Our new GPS indicates temperatures of 40°C (104°F). Everything we look at melts, and the road sticks to our tires. The heat makes us both irritable and frustration starts to mount like a bomb ticking under the surface. We try to find food in a village, but they only sell canned food. They don't even have carrots or onions. We remind ourselves that we often have trouble finding groceries on the first day, but it is yet another aggravation. "We'll figure something out; we always do," Zoë says. It sounds crazy like we have somehow forgotten the ins and outs of traveling. "Oh well, it is what it is," and we take some extra potatoes.

We cycle along endless roads. It looks a lot like the Chaco in Paraguay with thick vegetation on both sides of the road. When Olivier packs his panniers after lunch, he becomes frustrated. Because of the new gear, his bag won't close, and nothing fits like it used to. Zoë also feels a sense of unease, but most of all she is bothered by Olivier's subdued, taciturn attitude. Silently we cycle on. The irritation sinks into our muscles; we pedal harder and harder and say less and less. Zoë can't stand Olivier's grumpiness, but she understands perfectly what he is feeling because she feels it herself.

"What exactly is it that is making you so angry?" she finally asks.

Olivier's fingers tingle; he feels like stopping and emptying the entire contents of his panniers. The thought makes him even angrier. The bomb explodes. "We made bad choices," he shouts angrily. "Stupid trip, stupid stuff!"

"Honey, we're going to think of solutions," Zoë says and persists until Olivier calms down. 10 kilometers farther, it's Zoë's turn to break down and she cries. We park the bikes in the middle of the road and hold each other very firmly for a long time in silence.

"Sorry," Olivier says, and he holds Zoë even tighter. There we stand in the vast green forests, on a long endless road, fragile in each other's arms, barely a day after our restart. It's exactly what we need.

Laguna Bacalar is a long narrow lake in the southern Yucatán Peninsula, close to the border of Belize. It is nicknamed the "lake of the seven colors" because of the incredible shades of its crystalline waters, which are the result of a combination of coral reefs and underwater flora.

Belize doesn't have many roads. Close to the border of Guatemala, we can finally escape the main road and cycle on quieter dirt roads.
The official language in Belize is English, but closer to the border, almost everyone speaks Spanish.

An accident avoided

After one week in Mexico, we cross the border into Belize. We cycle on the busy main road that runs from the coast to the border of Guatemala. Normally, we prefer quiet roads with little traffic, but there is no alternative. We deliberately cycle in the middle of the road because this way, we have learned, cars slow down and pass us quietly. Today it's so busy that a traffic jam forms behind us. Just as we move to the shoulder, we hear a heavy crunching noise. Frightened, Zoë looks back and sees a black truck on the shoulder of the road, racing at breakneck speed in our direction. Our hearts are in our throats as we brace ourselves for the impact. But just before the truck hits Zoë's rear wheel, it swerves to the right, bounces in all directions, and plows toward a large billboard. By some miracle, the truck manages to dodge the obstacle and steer back on the road. Large piles of grass fly around and a thick cloud of dust is left behind.

During our trip, we have had some exciting moments that could have ended differently. But is that a reason to stay home? Our journey appears to be life-threatening for many people. Olivier's mother almost forbids us to start the Appalachian Trail. Poisonous snakes, aggressive wasps, large horseflies, ticks with Lyme disease, viruses in the water, large spiders, poisonous plants, limited drinking water, mosquitoes, black flies, extreme thunderstorms, getting lost in the endless forest, broken ankles, and hungry bears could all harm, or even worse, kill us. In the past 20 years, there have been only two fatal bear attacks. In the same 20 years, there have been more than 15,000 traffic-related fatalities in the Netherlands. There is always danger in our lives no matter what path we take.

We cycle on through the green hills of northern Guatemala. After two weeks of straight roads and flat landscapes, we finally hit some hills again. Women with long skirts walk along the road balancing large laundry baskets on their heads. When we take photos, they giggle shyly and cover their faces. In the villages, the men lean casually against walls and tables. They wear jeans with leather belts and wide-brimmed cowboy hats. They look at us from a distance but smile broadly when we take photos.

Two Jabiru storks fly over one of the lagoons in the Crooked Tree Wildlife Sanctuary. The sanctuary hosts endangered species like turtles, howler monkeys, and parrots, but the Jabiru stork is the area's most famous resident.

Mission impossible

"Impossible!" and "*no se puede*," says the teenager named Léon when we tell him about our plan. The more someone says that we can't do something, the greater our urge is to prove them wrong. We may be only fooling ourselves, but it is our motivation. We prefer intense hardship to long days at a leisurely pace. If we break a personal record, the day has been a complete success.

"Good luck," Léon says quickly as we finish our breakfast of rice and beans. We don't know what's in store for us. Google Maps gives us no information and the locals don't really know about the road to Mexico. They only know that the route "that way" is impossible for us. The first few kilometers aren't too bad, but then we see two concrete strips against the mountainside.

"Is that the road?" Zoë asks with wide eyes. With all of our resilience, we attack the concrete slab, but after 20 meters (66 feet) we come to a halt. We have to push our bikes up the 25 percent gradient. After three turns, we are both panting.

"This is going to be a long day," Olivier puffs. It is so steep we can hardly push our bikes up by ourselves. Together we push one bike around the turn and then fetch the other—turn, after turn, after turn. We then take a breath and go on. Breathe and go on. We are dripping with sweat. Our legs are sore from pushing, our arms ache, and the sun is getting hotter and hotter.

"7 kilometers since this morning," Olivier says after four hours. "We're almost at the top of the first section." Almost becomes 3 kilometers (2 miles), and that takes an hour and a half.

Eight hours later, we arrive at an unexpected stretch of asphalt. We are exhausted. "We did 15 kilometers in eight hours," Olivier says. "Yet another record," Zoë laughs.

Olivier looks at Zoë with admiration, "Two months ago you were on the operating table and now you're doing this. That's a miracle!" Physically, it's the toughest day since our journey has begun, and Zoë manages to do it as if nothing had happened in the meantime. "You're so mentally strong."

A smile appears on Zoë's face who is enjoying the fact that she can suffer again, push her limits, and perform at her top level. Our limits may not be where we think they are. And even when we think we've finally reached them, the next time we often find that they've moved again. We cycle and push for a few more hours until we see a small river. The water is freezing, but it's a godsend, just like our pasta dinner and our tent.

In the small town of Ixquisis, the teenager called Léon warns us that cycling will be impossible (opposite). Closer to the Mexican border, loose sand and steep concrete give way to a beautiful gravel road (above).

The small town of Flores is a great starting point for visiting the Tikal ruins. The old part of the city is located on an island in Lake Petén Itzá.

In El Rosario National Park, the park ranger assures us that it is safe to swim in the lake until 5 p.m.
After that, the crocodiles return to the lake from the swamps (opposite).

A New Muscle

Cycling across the Verdant Landscapes of Mexico

We leave calm Guatemala and cross the border back into Mexico, on the west coast this time. We discover deep gorges and waterfalls more beautiful than we've seen in nature documentaries. During lunch breaks, our tarp often provides the only protection from the scorching sun.

In the dry landscape, we switch to "sport mode" and get our motivation from challanging our bodies. We receive an invitation to join a group on Strava (an online platform where people share their sports activities). The group is full of top athletes and people who train for many hours a day like us. They do it to win races; we do it to explore. The Strava group makes a leaderboard at the end of every week. We win with the most elevation gain or the most hours on the bike, but we lag way behind when it comes to speed.

Tired, we arrive at Rodrigo's house. In the yard, two boys are playing with mangoes. "Come on in," says Mateo. "My father is still at school. Would you like something to drink?" We are sitting at the table when Rodrigo comes back home. "How old is your son?" Zoë asks. "Twelve," he smiles.

We talk for hours about our trip and his special life experiences. Many years ago, Rodrigo had the opportunity to study in the U.S. His host family welcomed him like he was their child. He is so grateful for this experience that he signed up for Warmshowers to do the same. We are the 300th cyclist he has hosted, but it feels like we are the first.

"There is a muscle in our body that is very difficult to train but has a huge efficiency," he says. Rodrigo looks at us expectantly, then points to his chest. "The heart?" Olivier asks. He shakes his head. "There is a very small muscle in there and it hurts a lot to train it. But the more you train this muscle, the happier you become." We hang on his every word.

"The giving muscle," he finally says. "We grow up in a society where we are selfish and greedy—that's why it hurts so much to give. Think of it as exercising. You fatigue the muscles, but afterward, it's satisfying," Rodrigo explains like it's scientific. "That's why we're so glad you're here, otherwise we wouldn't be able to train our muscles. To give, you don't need space in your home or wallet. To give, you need space in your heart."

Overwhelmed, we leave Rodrigo's house three days later. We forget our Strava group and decide to consciously train our giving muscles. Spontaneously, we offer our food to each other and let other travelers eat our meals. "Takers eat better, givers sleep better," we later read in a book. Our journey is on human power, but without the giving muscle of all the people along the way, we would never have made it this far.

In the dry season, southeastern Mexico is brown and barren. The Chiflón Falls area is a unique green oasis in the landscape and a wonderful place to sleep in a hammock. Since our restart in Mexico, we have added a hammock to our equipment for optimal sleeping comfort in tropical temperatures.

The hidden places in southern Mexico continue to surprise us. The Cascada el Aguacero is the last waterfall we encounter on our way north.

Southern Mexico is great for cycling. There is little traffic, the road quality is good, and the scenery is beautiful. Wild camping isn't always easy in the steep terrain with limited water availability, so we often search for camping spots in villages.

Unwanted visitors

After a few days of rest in Pachuca, we cycle farther north. We start late and arrive at a small village 50 kilometers (31 miles) farther on. We buy vegetables for dinner at a local store and ask where we can pitch our tent. "At the soccer field," says the salesclerk.

We cycle there and see a couple of football players resting with beers in their hands. "You can stay without any problems," they confirm our question. It's not the prettiest spot, but next to the field, there is a small building where we can hang our hammocks out of sight—a perfect spot. At 8 p.m., we get into our hammocks and fall asleep not much later.

In the middle of the night, we are startled awake. Five policemen with big machine guns shine flashlights into our eyes. Behind them, dozens of villagers stand in a semi-circle.

"What are you doing here?" asks a policeman.

"Sleeping, of course," is what we want to say, but we remain polite.

"You are not allowed to stay here," one of the officers says gruffly. "We're asking you to leave."

"Where should we go? It's the middle of the night." The big guns are intimidating. We aren't afraid that they will harm us, but the unfriendliness, the time of night, and the commotion are just too much. But there is a friendly man who tries to help. "You can hang your hammock at the *balneario,* the local swimming pool," he says.

We load our bikes into the cargo area of a pickup and squeeze in next to them. It seems like we're driving for miles, uphill, downhill, and all of this in the middle of the night in the back of an unknown pickup. We are only wearing windbreakers and are shivering from the cold. After far too long of a drive, we stop at a swimming pool complex with several hotels and partying guests. Do we have to hang the hammocks here, we think? "This is your room." The friendly man turns out to be the owner, and he offers us a hotel room.

It's the only time out of hundreds of times wild camping that we have had any issues, but it didn't turn out so bad after all.

Sugarcane is harvested by hand, and ancient grain silos dot the landscape in Chiapas (above). In a 150-kilometer (90-mile) radius around Mexico City, it is densely populated and not always easy to find quiet dirt roads such as this one (opposite).

Welcomed by Narcos

The border area between Mexico and the United States doesn't have a good reputation. We know it from the news and hear it daily from Mexicans. For two years, people have been warning us of the danger farther north. The Argentines say the Bolivians steal, the Bolivians say the Peruvians are thieves, and the Peruvians tell us that Ecuadorians are not to be trusted. "There" is always hearsay because they have never been "there" themselves. We learn to take it with a grain of salt and make our own rules. If we hear, "it is dangerous there," we just go, but when it changes to, "it is dangerous here," our ears prick up. The closer we get to the border of the U.S., the more often "there" changes into "here."

Fifteen minutes after we turn onto a country road, a car stops in front of us. The man makes a stop gesture. This has happened so often on our journey. Our instincts are trained to pick out the rotten apple that behaves "differently." This man falls into the good apple category, as does virtually everyone else on our journey. His gestures are serious but not suspicious. He has a message and doesn't just stop out of interest.

"You shouldn't be cycling here. It's dangerous," he says sternly. "When I saw you were a woman, I had to warn you. They kidnap women here. You have to cycle on the main road."

Zoë feels the warning in her whole body, all the way down to her toes. "I want to follow the main road, we're not taking any chances," she says. We change our plan and cycle the last 400 kilometers (250 miles) toward the U.S. on the main road.

El Castillo de la Salud, the Health Castle, is dedicated to the study, cultivation, and use of medicinal plants (opposite, top). A farm worker carries heavy buckets of freshly harvested zucchini (opposite, bottom). The Minas Viejas waterfalls in San Luis Potosí are perfect for a break or swim (above).

Just after we find a place to camp in a small field, a local farmer comes riding up on his horse to see who we are and what we want.
After a short talk, he permits us to spend the night on his land (opposite).

We are uncomfortable on our bicycles. People are cautious and greet us less than usual. Cars are driving slowly, and it feels suspicious. Long stretches without houses feel unpleasant. Along the way, we ask everywhere, "Is it dangerous here?" They shake their heads, "*no, no, tranquilo.*"

That night, we look for a place to camp along the main road. A man standing in his fenced-in yard says, "I would like to help you, but I have a family, and I don't know if I can trust you." Of course, we understand the man's dilemma, but it is still a stab in the heart not to be trusted.

Along the last few kilometers to the border, the main road is less busy. We assume it is because no one crosses the border. On the edge of the road, we spot a man standing in the grass. "Strange, what is that man doing there?" Zoë asks. "He probably works for the oil companies," Olivier suggests.

As we approach him, Zoë gets an uneasy feeling. She says a friendly hello to him, as she always does, but in her head, silent alarm bells start to ring. There is something about his demeanor that doesn't seem right. We remain silent, but the unease lingers in the air. Nothing wrong, we think until we see a second person standing in the grass. This time Olivier too begins to feel uncomfortable.

"This feels wrong, but turning around now would also look suspicious," Olivier says when he sees the strange man talking into his walkie-talkie. Before we can think things through, we see a third man who gestures for us to stop. We wave back enthusiastically and cycle on. Once we pass him, things go fast. A red jeep tries to block our way.

"What should we do!" shouts Zoë. "Stop!" Olivier shouts back. This isn't the time for playing games. Olivier dismounts and walks confidently to the open window, but inside he is trembling with fear.

"Where are you going?" "Where are you from?" and "How did you get here?" They are stern questions that must be answered.

Teotihuacán, about 40 kilometers (25 miles) from Mexico City, once was the largest city in the Americas. It is famous for the pyramids built in pre-Columbian America, especially the Pyramid of the Sun and the Pyramid of the Moon.

Olivier kindly answers them with the same enthusiasm as always. Secretly, he tries to look into the car, hoping he doesn't see a gun. The man stares at us with penetrating eyes.

"*Pasaportes,*" he says, gesturing with his fingers.

"Of course," Olivier says kindly. No, not the passports Olivier! How stupid, Zoë thinks. Without thinking, she stammers, "But you're not from the police." Oh God, what is she saying, Olivier thinks.

"No, that's not how it works here girl," the man says with a nasty grin. "We're in charge here. Passports, now!"

"Here you are," says Olivier and hands over his ID card. If they drive away now, we'll still have our passports and can cross the border.

"So, you're from Belgium," the man repeats when his companion has studied the ID card extensively. "Yes, look here," says Olivier and talks about our trip for the second time, while all he can really think about is running away.

"Okay, you can go," the man says as he hands back the ID card, "I'll command my men to let you pass," and he points to the walkie-talkie in the car.

We thank the men as if we had just had a pleasant conversation. "*Adios!*" We wave with a smile and continue our journey in silence—a silence that has never been so profound. Zoë knows what Olivier is thinking and Olivier what Zoë is thinking.

We cycle as fast as we can to the next village and say a friendly hello to all the men who already know who we are. We want to know how serious the situation is, but in the village people are silent. When we ask who those guys are, they look around anxiously and quickly turn around. We don't trust anyone.

Close to the border, we see normal policía again, heavily armed with machine guns on top of the jeeps. We find a place to sleep near the church. When we explain what just happened, the pastor says a little incredulously, "And they let you through?"

The area has been taken over by drug cartels. They are fighting and killing each other. A couple of years ago there was a war here. "People with guns walked the streets, and after 6 p.m., you couldn't go outside. It was a war zone. It's *tranquilo* now, but it could erupt at any moment."

Our American Dream

Riding from Texas to Georgia

Only one of three gates is open at the border. President Trump has shifted the priorities of customs officers from stamping passports to patrolling borders. Cars, cyclists, and pedestrians all have to go through that same gate. When it's our turn, there's already a line behind us. The officer looks sourly at our passports. He grabs the phone to call his boss, another official takes us inside. We are a little nervous and begin to wonder if they suspect us of something. The boss comes in and shakes our hands cheerfully.

"May we take a few pictures of you? We've never seen travelers on bicycles here before," the boss explains. There are signs that say, "It is strictly forbidden to take photos," but we pose for them anyway. "There will be an article about you in the border control newspaper," he says proudly.

Welcome to the United States of America. Smiling, we cycle into Texas. The contrast with Mexico is immediately noticeable. Suddenly, everything is supersized and orderly. There are traffic lights and stop signs where huge pickups with tinted windows actually stop. The streets are deserted and don't have colorful fresh fruit stalls or central plazas filled with people. We see large fast-food chains with long lines of cars in the drive-through, and driveways where only the mailbox betrays that someone lives there.

We cycle into the Recreational Vehicle Park in Victoria. The area is full of large RVs where most of the people live permanently. People living in RVs have a bad connotation in Europe, but we discover that behind every plastic camper door lies a special story.

We first meet Gregory at his camper at the back of the property on a perfectly mowed patch of grass. He is a giant man, weighing 127 kilos (280 pounds). He is wearing a bright yellow T-shirt and a cap that says, "Navy Veteran." He isn't your stereotypical active cyclist, but two years ago, he cycled 13,000 kilometers (8,000 miles) across the United States on a special tricycle. He weighed 181 kilos (400 pounds) when he left and lost more than 45 kilos (100 pounds) on his journey. He was treated everywhere, received hotel stays, and people even paid for his groceries. Since then, his camper has been open to any cyclist passing through.

People often tell us, "I could never do what you do," but Gregory is a wonderful example of what is possible. The journey he undertook with bad knees and excess weight is truly inspiring. His actions resound with an attitude of, "Yes, we can! There is always a way."

Our next host is Karen who invites us to a group home in Alexandria, Louisiana. We cycle up the driveway of a large mansion where several tricycles are parked. We ring the bell, and a young lady opens the door. Immediately, there are eight curious faces looking over her shoulder. Everyone is eager to meet us and hug us. The mansion is the home of eight women with disabilities. Karen is not home, but there is a long welcome letter in our bedroom. The table is full of treats: cookies made by the ladies in their own bakery, cereals, chips, and fruit. When Karen comes home, we see that she is more than the director of the organization. She is a valuable friend and mother to the ladies. Together we bake an apple pie, look through their photo albums, and eat pizza. Proudly, one by one, they show us their rooms and bikes.

"I don't usually invite cyclists here because I never know how they'll react," says Karen, "but they won't forget you." We won't forget them either.

Southern hospitality

"You need water. I'll buy you one," says the friendly man when he sees Zoë in front of the store.

"No, no, thank you, that's very kind, but I have water," Zoë replies. "Maybe you can help me with something else. We are looking for a place to pitch our tent."

For a week, churches have been our refuge for the night. Normally, we camp in the wild, or we ask for a spot in someone's yard, but we don't feel comfortable doing that in the southern states. Every property is marked with a "private property" sign. Even more off-putting are the supposedly funny signs that read, "If the dog don't get you, I will," and "Violators will be shot, survivors will be shot again."

We save our effort with houses and immediately cycle to one of the many churches in a town. We make sure to knock on the door before closing time and ask for a spot in the yard. They are incredibly helpful. Once we are even offered a motel room, and Pastor Arthur invites us to breakfast at a fancy cafe the next morning. Today, we are not so lucky; the church office is closed. The man who spontaneously wanted to offer us a bottle of water has an idea.

We follow him through a poor residential area and stop at Stefani's house. Her legs are full of tattoos, she has large bags under her eyes, and she seems incredibly chaotic. She says we can hang our hammocks in her yard. "Actually," she says, "there was a big rattlesnake in the yard yesterday, so maybe it would be better to sleep under the carport."

We don't feel quite comfortable. A man walks through the yard looking for his stolen bicycle, and children run out of the house all the time. We feel Stefani's genuine hospitality but also have an unsafe feeling. We realize that our uneasiness is a symptom of our prejudices. Prejudices are not innate. They are learned through politics, media, education, experiences, and fear. Movies and television make us think that drug addicts steal, it's dangerous in poor neighborhoods, and people who are in prison are all bad. Fortunately, we can unlearn our prejudices.

Our first impression of America is anything but the American dream that movies show us. There is a lot of obesity, fast food, drive-throughs, big pickups, and open carrying of firearms. The beautiful homes with neatly kept yards are by far the minority. There is a lot of poverty and drug problems. We see a country of extremes with huge contrasts between rich and poor, fat and thin, white and black, Trump supporters and adversaries. As apparent as the differences are, so are the similarities. All the Americans we meet are incredibly hospitable, generous, helpful, and enthusiastic.

Stefani tells us that she is a minister who helps drug addicts. She was an addict herself for over 20 years and has done a lot of bad things.

"That man who brought you to my house, Pete, I help him too. He got out of prison yesterday," she says.

As our tension drops, our guilt grows. We just prejudged this strong woman. Gratefully, we hang the hammocks under the carport and sleep well. Early in the morning, we find a bag of food on the chair with a note that says, "Some snacks for the road. Thanks for being here, and good luck on your journey."

Logistics angels

We knock on Novita's door in Atlanta exactly on the day we had aimed for on our schedule. Novita had reached out to us via Instagram and offered to host and help us. We will swap our bikes for backpacks in Atlanta and set off on a 1,000-kilometer (620-mile) hike along the Appalachian Trail. After the hike, we will take the train back to collect our bikes and other gear.

Without all the extra capacity of panniers, we now need to travel really light. We each pack two pairs of hiking shorts, two T-shirts, three pairs of socks, a sweater, and a raincoat. We will keep our computer and all other unnecessary weight in Novita's garage.

Before we even set off, we receive a message from Kim and Bob, our hosts at the other end of the trail. "It's crazy that you have to make such an effort to pick up your bikes. We'll get them for you," says Kim.

"What, they want to pick up our bikes 1,000 kilometers (620 miles) away?" We wonder if we understand the text correctly. That's a distance from the Netherlands to the south of France.

"Our son cycled 5,000 kilometers (3,100 miles) across the U.S. So many people helped him, and this is our way of paying it back. Besides, it's a good excuse to visit our family in Georgia," Kim explains.

All we have to do is complete the trail to be reunited with our bikes. Unbelievable.

The Deep South region of the USA is interesting to explore by bike, not specifically because of the landscapes but thanks to the people, culture, and rare roadside attractions like this gas station museum.

In Mississippi, this closed bridge saves us a 10-kilometer (6.2-mile) detour. Old bridges aren't removed but rather closed to traffic until they collapse (opposite).

The southern region of the U.S. doesn't have high mountains or spectacular national parks. The state and national parks in the area are often wetlands or lakes. Here we camp at Payne Lake in Alabama for the night.

Fifty Days of Rain

Hiking the Appalachian Trail

The Appalachian Trail is one of the most famous long-distance hikes in the United States. The trail is 3,500 kilometers (2,175 miles) long. We are "only" doing 1,000 kilometers (620 miles), and we know that will be enough of a challenge. To complete just this section, we have to climb the equivalent of Mount Everest five times. We are convinced that we can make it, but we are just as sure that it will be thoroughly difficult. The long road ahead has many high mountains. To reach the top, we must not overcome the mountain but ourselves.

"Springer Mountain, the southern terminus of the Appalachian Trail," is written on a large stone. Underneath a book is hidden in a metal box. Quickly we write our names in the book just like all the other hikers who start here.

"This is bizarre, we're going to hike 1,000 kilometers," Olivier laughs. We have cycled over 6,000 kilometers (3,700 miles) in the past three months, but we haven't walked much. Now we need to become hikers. We are in good shape, and we have all the gear we need, but our feet, legs, and shoulders aren't prepared. We feel that we can hike the trail as planned, but we know we have to remain realistic.

The weather has been beautiful for days, but today it's raining cats and dogs. It rains a lot in the Appalachian Mountains, so we keep psychologically preparing ourselves for the worst. Zoë's mental setback is the wind, for Olivier, it's the rain, but it doesn't matter. He walks through the torrential rain with a smile on his face. We follow the white rectangle trail markers painted on the trees. From now on, we will follow a path barely 50 centimeters (20 inches) wide that meanders through a green oasis. From the first few meters, it is extremely beautiful and completely different than any other hike we have ever done.

"Without all this rain, it wouldn't be so beautiful here," Olivier says. "You get less wet under the canopy." He walks through the rain with genuine delight. He listens to the hollow sound of falling drops and cheerful birdsong. "I'm already enjoying this, and the weather can only get better," he says.

Human minds have extraordinary power. If we can imagine something, our bodies can follow. Being mentally prepared for bad weather is just as important as being physically prepared. Imagining tough situations helps us endure them along the way. In fact, it can even help us overcome them. Ultimately, this is how we turn the situation around. Our setbacks become our motivation, easy moments become pleasant surprises, and sunshine becomes our reward.

A rare mountain-top vista in Georgia offers a spectacular view of the Appalachian Mountains. Most of the time, we walk in the forest, often referred to as "the green tunnel" by other hikers.

Traces of a past wildfire are apparent on this stretch of forest in South Carolina. Although there is plenty of rain in the Appalachian Mountains, wildfires happen (above). To prevent them, making a fire is only allowed in designated camping areas and three-walled shelters along the trail (opposite).

Trail magic

"In the wild forest we won't find friendly people who invite us in," Zoë says before we start. We are prepared for 100 percent independence, but after two nights in our tent, we wake up in Winton and Lisa's soft guest bed. We fry some eggs and have breakfast in the rocking chairs on the porch. Winton is awake early and practicing new songs on his guitar. He plays "Dust in the Wind."

"Do you guys have a trail name yet?" he asks. "From now on, you'll be called 'the Dust and the Wind.' You know why?" We both shake our heads. "Because you leave everybody fucking behind," he laughs loudly.

The official trail name needs to be inaugurated. We stand by the car and Winton says, "With the power given to me from the trees to the berries, I hereby declare Zoë and Olivier as the Dust and the Wind," symbolically knighting us with Zoë's hiking pole.

A week later, a third backpacker joins us. Simon, Olivier's brother, hasn't done many sports in recent months, but still flits up the hills. Everything obvious to us is new to him: the discovery of the white blazes on the trees, the green nature, the colorful reptiles on the ground, and counting in miles. We hike 20 kilometers (12.4 miles) on Simon's first day and pitch our tent in the forest. Simon has more hiking experience than we do, but we have our little habits after 10 days on the trail. We first wash in the stream, then set up the tent, and lie down for half an hour. Simon adapts without any problems. He only refuses to eat the peanut butter

sandwiches. We have divided our food among three backpacks. Olivier carries breakfast, Zoë lunch, and Simon dinner. We cook on one fuel stove, and fortunately, Simon has brought along his large cooking pot. A whole packet of pasta fits in it, and that's just enough for the three of us.

"I'm full," Simon says after two bowls. "Full?" we shout in unison. "In a few days, you'll be longing for more."

A week later, Simon licks out the pans and searches for the last crumbs in the package. "You know what I'm craving," he says after lunch, "a piece of fruit."

"I can name 10 things I would die for right now," Olivier adds. We're all longing for something that isn't there. The Appalachian Trail is a wild and remote environment where basic amenities are intentionally far away. It's the reason we hike here, and it's part of the experience.

"Hey what's that hanging in the tree?" Simon asks a couple of hours later pointing down the trail. They look like bananas. "No, it can't be true," he shouts for joy.

All day we have been alone on the trail, far away from the nearest house. We can't believe our luck. On the Appalachian Trail, they call it trail magic—finding exactly what you want the most when you least expect it. The entire trail is filled with hundreds of well-wishers who leave bags of food, set up coolers with cans of Coke, or park their trucks at a crossing and treat every hiker to a drink. They are trail angels, our guardian angels, just like our hosts Winton and Lisa.

A golden morning along the trail in North Carolina. The sun warms us, dries our clothes, gives us vitamin D, charges our power bank, and gives us light. It becomes one of our best travel companions throughout our entire journey.

Dreams are a choice

We hear a creaking noise above us. We stand still and hold our breath. After almost 300 kilometers (185 miles) on the trail, we still haven't seen a bear. We are about to enter the Smokey Mountains, and there are 1,500 black bears that live in the area.

If it is a bear, we should actually be making a lot of noise, but we want to see the animal first. We walk on quietly, searching the forest. We hear more crackling and turn around the next curve. The tension is palpable, and we try to avoid every branch. Then finally we see the source of the sound. An older man quietly trudges up the trail. It's Grinder, a 70-year-old man who is hiking the entire trail in sections. We met him yesterday, and today he is hiking up to the same shelter we are—almost 30 kilometers (18.5 miles)—with a heavy backpack. Grinder is his trail name because he slowly grinds out the miles. He has a clear goal. "I'm only 70," he says, "but I want to become the oldest man to hike the trail completely." The current record stands at 82. "Age is just a number," he says with a smile.

"I wish I had done that when I was young," we hear far too often. Excuses are very easy masks to hide behind. While traveling, we have met numerous people who were living proof that there should be no excuses when it comes to making dreams come true. We met a woman who left her family behind for her own three-month adventure and an eight-year-old girl who was hiking with her father for two weeks. We heard about blind people who have hiked the entire Appalachian Trail. We met cyclists who were traveling without money and young parents who cycled through South America with their children for a whole year. We met Gregory who cycled across America despite his excess weight and bad knees. They were all normal people who could have used the same familiar excuses. Instead, they have taught us that you don't need to be athletic, young, or rich to make your dreams come true.

Around 4 p.m., we arrive at the shelter. It is mandatory in the Smoky Montains to sleep in one of the open huts—partly because of the bears, and partly to protect the environment. We have time to bathe in the stream and rest. The sky turns black and a thunderstorm rumbles in the distance. We wait with our supper until Grinder stumbles into the shelter, exhausted and soaked. He left his fuel stove at home to save weight. He is used to cold meals, but now he enjoys the bowls of pasta we serve him. He thanks us with trail stories, crawls into his sleeping bag satisfied, and is on the trail again at 6 a.m., far ahead of us. In an hour or two, we will catch up with our old Grinder.

The Great Smoky Mountains along the Tennessee–North Carolina border are one of the most beautiful parts of the southern Appalachian Trail. The name comes from the natural fog that often hangs over the range.

Hikers' marathon

At 5:30 a.m., Olivier's watch vibrates. The only sound is the flowing water in the river, but otherwise, it's peaceful. The forest is still asleep, as is Zoë.

"Wake up, *princesa*," Olivier whispers, "big day."

"Hmm, what, what day is it?" mutters Zoë.

"We're trying the hikers' marathon."

"How far is it?" Zoë asks. She didn't want to know the distance, but she was up for the challenge.

"48 kilometers" (30 miles).

For once, we don't take the time for oatmeal, but quickly put energy bars in our mouths and start hiking.

"Six o'clock," Olivier says, and he starts his watch.

We've been on the trail for over a month and have covered 700 kilometers (435 miles). Simon has helped us over halfway, but we have to rely on our own motivation for the second half. Yesterday we met a young woman with freckled cheeks. Last year, she wanted to hike the entire trail. She lost 25 kilos (55 pounds) in three months. She ate only twice a day and usually no more than a package of instant noodles. That's only about 400 calories. She suffered a brain hemorrhage and needed six months to recover. Proper nutrition is incredibly important, but even though we try hard, we never get enough calories. In Atlanta, after cycling 6,000 kilometers (3,700 miles), Olivier weighed just 63 kilos (138 pounds), 3 kilos (6.6 pounds) under his normal weight.

We walk briskly all day. We only take short breaks, nibbling from our trail mix. At 6:20 p.m., we throw off the packs and plop down on the ground, happy to be done and especially longing for dinner. We have walked for over 12 hours, covered almost 3,000 meters (9,800 feet) of elevation gain, and burned about 5,000 calories.

It is the last day before our resupply and our evening meal consists of simple pasta with tomato sauce—800 calories per person. Olivier opens the valve of the fuel stove, takes out his lighter, and lights the stove. "Wooow shit!" he says jumping two meters in the air. The stove, the tube, and the bottle of gasoline all catch fire. We watch the fireball from a safe distance. We wait for it to explode, but it eventually just burns down. Olivier throws dirt over it to make sure the fire is fully extinguished. It was a museum piece, inherited from Zoë's parents, but now it has let us down. Growling, our stomachs ask when dinner will be served.

The next day we arrive in Damascus, nicknamed Trail Town USA. This is where the annual Appalachian Trail Festival takes place. Today the village of 800 inhabitants is peacefully calm. We rush to an outdoor store with our museum piece in hand. The owner, looks at us sternly, "You guys shouldn't cook with regular gasoline; that doesn't work." We have been doing this for three years, but he is convinced that our MSR stove isn't the cause of the problem. He takes the stove outside, empties the bottle in the gutter, and fills it with white gas. This time it's the shop owner who jumps two meters in the air. Terrified, he straightens his cap and walks back into the store. When he comes out, he has a brand-new stove in his hands. "So, they do wear out. Happy trails guys. I hope this one lasts 20 years too."

Every year, over 3,000 hikers attempt to thru-hike the entire Appalachian Trail in one go. Only 25 percent of the hikers succeed. Most thru-hikers start in Georgia in the spring and finish in Maine in fall, taking an average of six months.

In Pennsylvania, a Mennonite family invites us to their farm and allows us to take photos—an extremely rare opportunity because Mennonites usually refuse any kind of technology in their culture (opposite).

Everything comes to an end

Suddenly we are at the asphalt road that marks the end of the trail for us. We have hiked over 1,000 kilometers (620 miles). Our legs and hearts feel like hiking all the way to the end, to the top of Mount Katahdin. We feel in top shape but also look worn out. Olivier in particular looks like a wild man; his beard has never been so long, and his eyes are hollow. Zoë looks a lot better with healthy tanned skin and round cheeks. We conquered our personal challenges and the high mountains, helped by trail magic and inspiring people along the way.

A thousand kilometers once sounded like an impossible distance, but now we are already dreaming of more. Proud and sad, we arrive in Pearisburg, where Kim and Bob pamper us in their warm nest.

The bikes are in their garage, but we have to psych ourselves up to get back in the cycling saddle again. We cycle through Virginia, Maryland, Pennsylvania, and New York to get to the canoe trail.

A Heavy Burden

Hitting the Northern Forest Canoe Trail

A few months ago, we were discussing our new challenges. "What do you think will be the toughest part?" Olivier asked. "Hiking," Zoë said confidently. "Canoeing," was Olivier's answer.

Now we are about to start the Northern Forest Canoe Trail, 1,200 kilometers (750 miles) in a canoe, a quarter upstream, over 100 kilometers (60 miles) of portaging, big lakes, and wilderness without any canoeing experience. This canoe trip is described as one of the most challenging in the world. Barely 50 people start it every year, and only about 10 of them make it to the end.

We deliberately choose new challenges and push our limits, but we do this step by step. Extreme is relative when we look at the mountains we have climbed, the distances we have covered, and the challenges we have completed. "20 kilometers a day and we will have 1,000 kilometers before we know it," concludes Olivier.

On Saturday morning, we are at the canoe launch site ready to go. John, the owner of the canoe company in Old Forge, has helped us prepare for a successful trip. Our canoe is half in the water and half on the sand. It is filled with waterproof bags and a foldable cart we will use for portages, the overland transports to get to the next body of water or around obstacles in the river. There is room for a lot more stuff, but with all the portages in mind, we want to travel as lightly as possible.

We get into the canoe and put the paddles in the water. We begin a rhythmic stroke that we try to execute in synchrony. Our canoeing experience is limited to a single afternoon, but we are able to make a reasonably straight line as we paddle farther and farther up the lake.

There is no easing ourselves in. On the first day, we have two portages, and on the second day, we actually need to carry everything on our shoulders. It is common for canoeists to do several portages to transfer all their gear. We want to carry everything in one go. It's heavier, but also more efficient, we think. We prefer to suffer once at 100 percent instead of twice at 80 percent. Olivier takes the food bag and the canoe. We tie the life jackets to the chairs. Zoë takes the bag with sleeping gear on her back with water shoes and water bottles on the side. She carries the gray camera bag in one hand and the cart in the other. The total weight is 100 kilograms (220 pounds), and we each carry half. The portage is about 1.5 kilometers (1 mile); a monster distance to cover with 50 kilos (110 pounds) of awkward luggage on our backs. We try to walk as fast as we can, but they are hard steps on shaky legs.

Nearly a quarter of the Northern Forest Canoe Trail is upstream. After Lake Champlain, the trail continues on the Missisquoi River, which includes stretches of extremely challenging rapids.

The Adirondack Park, known as The Adirondacks, is an enormous wilderness area with over 10,000 lakes and almost 50,000 kilometers (31,000 miles) of rivers. The Mud Pond carry is one of the toughest portages of the entire trip.

"Een twee drie vier vijf zes zeven, zo gaat het goed, zo gaat het beter, alweer een kilometer," Olivier mumbles a Dutch nursery rhyme, but it doesn't help. He has to take the canoe off his shoulders.

"Zoë!" he shouts, but Zoë is not there. "Zoë, I can't hold it any longer!" He rests the back tip of the canoe on the ground, but that doesn't ease the pain. Frantically, he searches for a rock or a tree on which to place the front tip of the canoe. He finds a large rock, drops to his knees, and places the tip of the canoe on it. He sprints to Zoë. She is stumbling across the muddy path with her arms tensed, her teeth clenched, and her hair tousled. Quickly, he brings over the gray camera bag and says, "Wait, hold on a second. This has to be on film. Walk back a little."

"Are you crazy!" screams Zoë, but she walks back knowing it would be perfect for our film.

A leap of faith

A leap of faith is the best way to learn something, and the most challenging, we think. We would learn the techniques of canoeing on the way, and after 50 days, we would be experienced canoeists. Good plan we think until we see our first rapids. The water level is low and all we see are large rocks among the fast-flowing water. Beforehand, experienced canoeists gave us some tips. Follow the stream with the most water, sit on your knees, and paddle as slowly as possible without stopping. We get out of the canoe and look for the best way.

"To the right of that big rock, then immediately to the left, and then to the left of that rock," Zoë says, "or maybe better to the left of the big rock and stay to the left." We can see 30 meters (100 feet) ahead and then the river curves. "Oh well, we'll see," says Olivier, "as long as we don't scratch the canoe."

"We'll see;" we do that so often on our journey. Often, we blindly follow our intuition, but will it be correct? How do we navigate rapids with such little experience? Is the water level too low to paddle? Is there too much wind to cross the lake? What do we do then?

"Let's try it. You have to indicate right or left, and keep paddling," Olivier says.

We get back in the canoe, tie down all the bags, and let the water guide us. From the top of the stone, the water didn't seem to be flowing fast, but once in the canoe we quickly approach

Browns Tract Inlet is a beautiful meandering river with the occasional beaver dam as an obstacle (top). Two otters play alongside our canoe for an hour in the Allagash Wilderness Waterway (above).

that first big rock. "Left, left!" shouts Zoë. "Paddle right!" shouts Olivier in return.

We just manage to avoid the first big rock and we are already heading to the next one. Was it left or right of this rock? There is no time to think. We have to decide in a blink of an eye. A decision based only on intuition. We wanted a leap of faith, didn't we? Zoë sees the best route just in time and shouts, "Now, right, right, right!" We are able to avoid the second large rock and prepare for the next maneuver.

Kkkrrrrrrrrrrrkrkrkrkrkrrrrrrrrrr. "Oh shit! That's a really big scratch," Zoë curses disappointedly.

We don't have much time to process because the rocks keep coming one after another. We hit a few more hidden rocks, but for the first time ever, we did quite well. We didn't tip over, we didn't lose a paddle, there is no hole in the canoe, and we are a little more experienced.

A day later, we pull our canoe through the Saranac River. The water is so low that we cannot paddle. We walk through the water, but the canoe still scrapes over the stones. We stumble and curse over the slipping stones.

"What would experienced canoeists do now?" Olivier wonders aloud. "They won't completely ruin their boat," Zoë says with conviction. "I don't think so either."

We stumble to the riverbank, put the canoe on the cart, and begin a 20-kilometer (12.5-mile) walk to Lake Champlain. We will need to cross the thirteenth-largest lake in the U.S. to continue north. Our guidebook warns us that the wind can pick up unexpectedly and waves can be so high that canoes tip over. This time we really need to make a smart and safe choice. We will leave early when the wind is calm. We set the alarm for 5:30 a.m.

"This wasn't part of our plan," Olivier says when he pokes his head out of the tent. We are standing in our host Bill's yard overlooking the big lake. The wind is blowing strong and there are already waves on the water. Bill is in the kitchen preparing bagels and eggs for us. His weather station says the wind will start blowing harder in an hour. From Bill's house, we have to cross 3 kilometers (1.9 miles) of open water. We decide to go, and if it is too dangerous, we will turn back.

The wind is blowing hard at our side, and there are three large ferries sailing—a bonus risk factor. We paddle at full speed, both on the right side of the canoe. As we get farther from land, the wind blows even harder. The ripples in the water turn into whitecaps. By now there is no turning back. The waves are high, and it is almost impossible to keep the canoe in a straight line. Our canoe feels puny on the turbulent lake. The water sloshes into the boat and Zoë feels the blows of the waves in the front. Still, we feel we have the boat under control, and Olivier feels like a tough sea dog, without the seasickness this time. All we can do is paddle as hard as we can to get to the other side before the wind gets even stronger. We only dare breathe a sigh of relief when we are a few meters from land. We were on the edge, but now we know where our limits lie.

The North Branch Moose River in Old Forge, New York, is a maze. To find our way through, we need to stay on the main stream, but just as often, we get stuck and have to try another way out.

A canoe obstacle course

"You are here in the wrong season," we hear as we walk along another nearly dried-up river. It is the umpteenth time in our journey that people have told us this. We left Amsterdam in the fall, cycled in Colombia in the rainy season, and now we are doing the canoe trip when the water level is at its lowest. It means more portaging and more obstacles like beaver dams, fallen trees, and overgrown bushes. For us, it's all fun and surprises. It's like an obstacle course.

On the third day, we climb over the first beaver dams. This was only a small one we later learn. We leave early because we know a long day awaits us. Our guidebook warns us of a maze among the marshes. The waterways between the plants move and channels can misleadingly run to a dead end. The trick is to follow the mainstream, which has just a little more flow than the rest of the bog. We look at the direction of aquatic plants underwater, but nevertheless, we quickly get lost. It is difficult to navigate because the canoe sits so low in the water and the tall grass makes it difficult to see. The GPS helps somewhat, but where there was a route last year, this year there is none.

After an hour of wandering back and forth, we finally find the hidden route in the maze and breathe a sigh of relief, but just a little too soon. Two turns farther on, we are at a standstill again. A gigantic beaver dam looms in front of us blocking our way. We get out and find the lowest spot of the dam where we can push the canoe over a small waterfall. The whole operation takes about fifteen minutes, and we get back on board satisfied when the job is done.

The beavers have built a serious obstacle course for us. It takes us all day to navigate 18 dams, and we have to look for a campsite when it's almost dark. "I hope tomorrow will be a little less challenging," Olivier says in the evening in the tent, but the next day we have to navigate 15 more dams.

No obstacle course is meant to be easy, and there is no such thing as the wrong season. Every season has its advantages and disadvantages. Right now, fall is the perfect season in many ways. There are hardly any bugs, the water is warm, we enjoy the Indian Summer, we find blueberries everywhere, and the lower water level gives us more variety and adventure.

We've already learned a lot together, but the canoe takes us to the next level. From captaining our own ship, we now paddle as two captains on the same ship.

For the first time in a long while, we will paddle downstream. We can't wait, and despite the rain, we both have smiles on our faces while canoeing. The force of the water drags us along and we paddle at a record speed of 12 kilometers (7.4 miles) per hour. One rapid follows another. With Olivier in the back and Zoë on the lookout, we shout commands to each other. There are no dangerous rocks on our course this time, but still, we have to maneuver the boat back and forth. There is just enough water, but only if we stay in the right trench. If we misread the water once, we'll be stuck on the bottom, but that doesn't happen. We feel like a winning team guiding the boat through every obstacle in our path.

Two days later, we find ourselves in front of the Little Spencer Stream. It will be the biggest obstacle of our canoeing adventure, and Zoë isn't exactly prepared for that. Our guidebook tells lies: you will need to get out of your canoe every now and then. Her motivation sinks when she sees the dry river. She keeps quiet, hoping for better, but when that doesn't happen, the irritation

We just find the exit from the Clyde River maze (above) and enjoy an easy section on the Canadian part of the trail (opposite).

begins. The stones are too slippery to carry everything at once, so we grab half of our gear and slog to the next bend. Olivier balances the canoe over the slippery stones, while Zoë follows, cursing and slipping. After 500 meters (1,640 feet) of clumsy stumbling, we are exhausted. Zoë radiates unhappiness and irritation.

"What's wrong?" Olivier keeps asking. "Aaggrrr, this sucks! We should go through the forest" she says.

We try to maneuver the canoe through the forest, but it soon becomes too dense for the long canoe, and the river is the only option. It takes an hour and a half to cover only a kilometer. Zoë is about to explode.

"How long is it to the lake?" asks Zoë angrily.

"Twelve and a half kilometers."

"What! We will never make that! Look how slowly we're progressing."

"Come on Zoë, we have to work as a team, you're no use to me like this," says Olivier in vain.

Zoë moves to the front of the canoe. Irritation courses through her body, but she knows this is not fair to Olivier. She needs to get it off her chest, but she can't. She doesn't know why, but Olivier's attempt to get her in a better mood annoys her immensely.

"Okay, if you don't say anything about my temper, I'll behave." Olivier looks at her and starts laughing. Then Zoë also has to laugh. "We're crazy for doing this," she says. "Sorry about that. Thank you for staying so positive."

We are a team again. The two of us work our way forward kilometer by kilometer. The dry river is no longer a frustration, but a motivation. The slippery stones—not an irritation, but a challenge.

Like the well-known adage says, "Life is not about waiting for the storm to pass, but about learning to dance in the rain." Two captains in charge of one ship. We make it work.

Dealing with hardships

- Suffering is part of life. We need it to become mentally and physically stronger. Real satisfaction is achieved by overcoming suffering.
- We train our endurance, patience, and perseverance by holding on just a little longer than last time. This applies to physical endeavors as well as mental challenges.
- Whatever the season, we have the ability to make ourselves comfortable and safe.
- There is always a solution. We should focus on the new opportunity instead of the problem.
- It is not necessary to be top fit and fully prepared to start; the journey is the training. We know that the first three days are the toughest. After that, endurance grows, and our bodies begin to get used to the exercise.

The sunset conjures beautiful fall colors on the hills along the U.S.–Canadian border (opposite). The very last portage of the trail goes around Allagash Falls, the end of the Allagash Wilderness Waterway. From here, it's only 70 kilometers (43 miles) to the end in Fort Kent, Maine (above).

Polar Explorers

Skiing through Canadian Winterscapes

For the last five days, we have been floating downstream to our final destination on an ever-widening river. Suddenly, there are houses next to the water and we see an occasional car. We would like to canoe for hundreds of kilometers more, but winter is knocking at the door. We paddle as slowly as possible, but the river inevitably pushes us to the end. We don't have a plan yet, but we do have a host family waiting for us.

We sit outside on the porch at Carl and Pat's house in Fort Kent, the town at the end of our canoe trip. We are in sportswear with a healthy red glow on our cheeks. All morning we were with Carl on roller skis, a summer sport for cross-country skiers who train at the biathlon center. Carl is the president and coaches the athletes.

"This would be a cool way to travel," Zoë says enthusiastically, but then focuses again on the upcoming winter. We have been dreaming about a skiing adventure but have no idea how it works, if there are trails, and what kind of skis we need. Carl is a biathlon trainer and ski expert, so we are in the right place to learn. Zoë asks if it is possible to tie ski routes together, and she talks about the possibilities she has researched. Carl looks approvingly at Zoë's plans.

"You can also follow the Saint Lawrence in Québec," Carl says. "There's no road, but people live there. In the summer they can only travel by boat, but in the winter, they ride snowmobiles from town to town," and he draws the map in the air.

We take our computer; Olivier finds a video and presses play. Vast white plains, remote villages, and wild nature glide across the screen. We don't say a word, but goose bumps prickle down our arms. "Are we going to do this?" Zoë asks, full of adrenaline.

Carl follows our gazes and smiles. One morning outside and a one-minute video determine the rest of our adventure. We're going to ski for three months in Canada and then cross Europe on roller skis.

Once upon a time, ideas like sailing across the Atlantic or canoeing through the wilderness were madness and naive. It is not luck or coincidence that brings us here. It is thanks to frequently asking the question, "What are we going to do next?" That's how we learn to find our ideas, dreams, and desires. When we tell our story to people, there is always one among them who says, "Oh, I have an idea too."

Along La Route Blanche, there are regularly spaced emergency shelters that offer protection from rough weather. Between Kegashka and Blanc-Sablon, there are 23 of them, spaced 10 to 15 kilometers (6 to 9 miles) apart. They all have their number in black on top of the roof.

A quiet day among all the stormy days with blizzards in Baie-Johan-Beetz, Canada (above). Blizzards can provide large amounts of hard-packed snow, so a snowblower is a mandatory machine in this region (opposite).

A life of outdoor longevity

Carl and Pat go on a two-week vacation in Spain. We take care of the house, the animals, and Carl's parents, Lucien and Marie, who live next door. But actually, it's more like Lucien and Marie look after us. When the first snowstorm passes, Lucien sees us shoveling snow on the long driveway. A few minutes later, he drives by with his small tractor and blows all the snow away.

"Were you really planning to do it all by yourself?" he laughs exuberantly. The storm has wreaked havoc in the forest and several trees are lying across the ski trails. In the afternoon, Lucien picks Olivier up with the all-terrain vehicle. Lucien cuts a fallen tree with the chainsaw and drags it aside. After that, he's on to the next tree and the next for hours on end. In the basement, Lucien builds bicycle racks and chops his own wood. Lucien is 94 years old, and he still skis.

Our view of America has changed in recent months. Here in the North, we find an outdoor culture with many active people. Lucien takes the crown, and his son Carl has inherited his genes. There is a mug in their house with a saying: "Keep the house clean by staying outside." It is both the family's motto and a motto for healthy living. But it's more than that. Lucien and Carl and other volunteers have put in hundreds of hours to build the biathlon center. Fort Kent has a population of barely 4,000, but there is a great sense of community in the village. Everybody knows their neighbor and helps each other.

Three days before we leave, there is a celebration at the Outdoor Center. It is the annual meeting with a special item on the agenda. Behind the lectern, a large wooden plaque is hidden under a sheet. It is Carl, the president of the club, who gets to surprise his father with a grand gesture. Slowly, the plaque which says "Lucien J. Theriault Stadium" is revealed. The biathlon stadium, which has hosted numerous events and World Cup competitions, has been named to honor Lucien. He rises from his chair humbly. He doesn't like the attention and is visibly emotional.

The room is silent as Lucien clears his throat. "Thank you, Carl and all of you. And I know who is going to hang the plaque." The audience bursts into laughter.

The bay in La Romaine, Québec, is half frozen (above). Wildlife tracks abound, but we hardly see the animals themselves. Only birds occasionally show themselves, like the ruffed grouse, which, like us, enjoys the soft morning sunlight (opposite, bottom).

Before reaching La Route Blanche, the only asphalt road in this area often parallels our trail. Saint-Lawrence Bay lies south of the road, and to the north, there is nothing but wilderness.

Winter cycling shorts

We have been staying with Carl and Pat for two months. Meanwhile, it is early December and winter has arrived. Our visas expires tomorrow, so we really have to leave. Canada is literally just across the river. Carl cycles with us across the bridge. We get stamps in our passports that allow us to stay in Canada for up to six months. Then we cycle our first few meters in Canada together with Carl.

The 400 kilometers (250 miles) to Québec City is our first real test of cycling in winter conditions. This morning the thermometer showed -15°C (5°F), but Olivier still decides to cycle in shorts. The ground is covered in a thick blanket of snow and large sheets of ice float in the river. The road is snow free and a warm winter sun makes the temperature pleasant. Two heavy trailers filled with far too many things bump around behind us. We will use the trailers for our next adventures on skis and skates. We still have a lot of canoe equipment and a lot of new gear for the harsh winter in Québec. Carl bikes quietly ahead of us while we feel like old tractors. It's not more tiring than usual, we just go much slower for the same effort.

Winter food

We go to the supermarket in Québec with a special mission—to reinvent our food system. We investigate almost every product in the supermarket. In a few weeks' time, we'll be skiing through a remote area in winter conditions. Anything containing liquid will freeze. The simple meals that we always cook are suddenly too complex. We do have one big advantage: our food won't spoil in the frigid cold conditions.

A few days later, we buy two shopping carts full of food. We buy dozens of bags of trail mixes, thirty packs of chocolate, boxes of energy bars, bags of powdered milk, pounds of oatmeal, a tower of packaged tortillas, and masses of vegetables. We are staying with Francis, a member of a local outdoor association. His house is our base camp. For a whole day, we cook mushroom risotto, rice with beans, and pasta sauce. We spread the dishes out on the drawers of a food dehydrator, wait 12 hours, and divide the meals into individual Ziploc bags. When the meals are ready, we dry kilos of vegetables. Most vegetables contain more than 90 percent water. A kilogram (2.2 pounds) of carrots weighs only 100 grams (3.5 ounces) after dehydrating.

With crammed bags and boxes, we walk to the post office. We divide the dried meals into boxes together with the nuts, breakfast, chocolate, tortillas, parmesan cheese, and energy bars. Our supplies take up almost half the post office when we spread them out on the floor. Each box contains a five-day supply of food that we send to the villages we will ski past. We send two packages to some post offices to cover longer distances. The remainder goes into the sled, our supply for the first 10 days. We hope it's tasty.

The impossible becomes possible

In Portugal, we met another world cyclist for the first time—Marlène, a young woman from France who cycled from the North Cape to Gibraltar. Alone, as a woman, cycling for six months, we couldn't believe it. What a superhuman. Three years later others call us the same.

We stay with Jonathan and Caroline for the last few days before our departure. We met them in Peru and, like many people we have met, they said, "if you ever come to our town, you have a home." The night before we leave, we sit with Jonathan in front of the fireplace for a long time and crawl into bed late. Next to our bed, our ski clothes are folded in anticipation of our next adventure. As of tomorrow, we will be sleeping outside at the mercy of the brutal winter. We are embarking on an adventure that seemed impossible for a long time. In our minds, polar explorers are experienced adventurers born in countries with harsh winters. They are superhumans equipped with the most expensive packs, and they prepare for their trip for months. We were born in the wrong country and have no experience with winter, but tomorrow we will begin our own journey.

Over the past three years, we have tried so many new things we thought we wouldn't be able to do. Biking, sailing, canoeing, and hiking—everything was new to us, yet everything ended well. It gives us confidence that we can overcome new challenges without being experts. We learned a little bit of canoeing, biking, hiking, and sailing, but we learned intensively to live outside, to challenge ourselves, to overcome obstacles, to travel together, and to persevere. That experience gives us the confidence to take on unknown adventures. Yet this time the preparation is much more extensive. We needed four days for hiking, eight days for canoeing, and three months for this adventure. We know we will encounter difficulties and surprises. Some people tell us we are crazy, while others think it is great. We give a presentation at the University of Québec. At the end, we ask, "Who thinks we'll make it?" Three-quarters of the hands went up in the air.

At 8 a.m. the next day, we get into the car and Jonathan takes us to the start of our trail. Fascinated, he and his son Albert watch. A steep climb immediately awaits us, so we put the climbing skins on the bottom of our skis. They ensure that we can glide forward without slipping backward. We connect our sleds to our hip belts and take a good look at each other. That doesn't look bad, we think. Zoë smiles, this is what we have dreamed of but always seemed impossible. The smile is much more than a smile, it is the realization that we are a little crazy and that's our normal.

A lone ice-fishing hut on a small lake near Saint-Augustin in Québec. Much of the population works in the fishing industry, but that season doesn't start until April. In winter, there is plenty of time for ice fishing.

La Route Blanche is a popular route for snowmobilers, but the route we follow up to the trail is hardly ever used. The extreme temperatures take a toll on our equipment and impede our progress.

A bad start

Olivier presses the GPS to start. "Bleep, bleep, training started." Zoë, meanwhile, has already done 50 meters (165 feet) and Olivier sees that things are going smoothly. The climbing skins do their job. The slope is steep, but step by step we move forward. We drag the weight of our sleds behind us, about 50 kilos (110 pounds) per person. It is snowing lightly, and the temperature is around freezing—warm for January. We start with our jackets and hats on, but soon Olivier is skinning up in just a T-shirt with sweat dripping off his nose.

We know the elevation profile and know that we have to climb a lot of steep hills for the first three weeks. It scares us a little, but no more than any of the other challenges have. We'll make up the miles as we ski along the coast, we think, but the trail is getting steeper, and it's becoming harder to keep our momentum. Every time Zoë looks back, she sees Olivier pulling the sled uphill with all his might. Sometimes he stops and looks up, and she sees the look of concern in his eyes. She knows he's not enjoying it yet. The skiing is fantastic, and the scenery is beautiful, but in his head, the planning is already messed up, and we are running behind schedule. Olivier never gets stressed unless he's running late. We are barely moving. Even the climbing skins start to lose their grip under so much weight. It's still a long way to the top, but then there will be a descent, we think.

"We'll see what it's like after five days if this is madness," Olivier tells himself encouragingly. It's only the first day, so it's normal that it feels tough. 50 meters (165 feet) farther on, we are at a complete standstill. We can't pull the weight of the sled up anymore. Olivier is bent over his ski poles in the middle of the trail and needs all his strength to keep from sliding backward. Our legs are shaking as we stand still. The trail looks more like a white wall.

Brrrrrrmmmmmmm. For a moment, Olivier panics. He can't take a step because he'll lose his grip. We know how fast snowmobiles drive. The man sees us just in time and comes skidding to a halt, 5 meters (16 feet) in front of Olivier. That was close, but this is life-threatening. We have only just started, but we are both thinking the same thing. This time the decision is made quickly, faster than ever before. The slopes are too steep and too dangerous. It's senseless and irresponsible. There is only one right choice. We turn around.

We slide carefully back down to the start losing our smiles on the descent. We replace the skis with wheels and walk back to Jonathan's house. We don't say a word, and the impact of the decision grows larger between us with each step. Disappointment rolls silently down our cheeks. We curse in silence and are deeply disappointed. We curse our own mistakes in preparation. If only we had listened to our feelings when we saw the elevation profile on our computer. But that same feeling brought us here to the start of a new challenge. Zoë puts on a smile when we knock on Jonathan's door and says, "We're back."

In the afternoon, we contemplate new plans, and we decide to restart farther north where the mountains aren't so high. Our confidence has been shaken but not our motivation. By falling, we learn to get up. We need setbacks to truly appreciate positive moments. We have learned that this path with this equipment at this time is not right for us. We have also learned that sometimes a new plan is the best answer. Tomorrow we will be back at the start and turning a new page.

Freezing cold

Our eyes open, and we look at the yellow tent liner that is full of frost. Our noses are cold, and our warm breath immediately freezes in the air. The mouths of our sleeping bags are covered with a white layer of ice, but inside they are toasty. The zippers are closed and the hoods are wrapped around our heads. We still have our beanies on. The most comfortable part of winter camping has just passed, the 12 hours in a warm sleeping bag. Last night we peed twice before crawling into our sleeping bag hoping to sleep through the night. While Zoë slept like a marmot, Olivier woke up at 5 a.m. with a bloated bladder. Then he had to choose between an uncomfortable couple of hours in the warmth or suffering for five minutes while peeing in the freezing cold wearing only his thin layer of thermal underwear. The brief pain won out. The thermometer read -29°C (-20°F).

Our ski clothes are at the foot of the sleeping bag. With our feet, we try to distinguish a pair of socks from gloves. We put on as many clothes as possible in the warm sleeping bag. We have to open the sleeping bag to put on our shirts. With every inch that we unzip the bag, more cold air gets in. As quickly as possible, we put on our woolen shirt, but in all the fury, we touch the yellow tent liner and sweep a layer of ice around. We are constantly in each other's way, and it takes far too long to get warmly dressed. We growl when either of us accidentally touches the tent. We need a better system. Outside the tent, we pat the frost off the sleeping bags and try to squeeze the large volume of down back into the stuff sack. The cold makes everything hard and less flexible.

While Zoë packs the tent, Olivier makes breakfast. He mixes some water with powdered milk and cocoa, and heats the pan over a weak flame before adding the oatmeal-granola blend. For a moment the pot is warm, but at -20°C (-4°F) everything cools very quickly. When we are halfway through the pan, the bottom part is already frozen stiff.

"We need another solution for the morning," Olivier says with his half-frozen spoon.

We seem almost ready to leave, but every action that is normally so easy represents a new challenge. We can barely squeeze the toothpaste out of the tube, the bristles of the toothbrush are frozen, and the sunscreen is one block of ice. Finally, we swap our winter shoes for our ski boots. Although it was -10°C (14°F) all day yesterday, we still sweat in our boots, resulting in a white layer of frost on the inside. The zipper is frozen solid, and the boots seem three sizes too small. We blow warm breath into the opening to thaw them out and squeeze our feet in millimeter by millimeter. When we finally get in, our toes are frozen. With a pained grimace, we jump around and kick ourselves warm. Although we are still cold, we swap our warm down jackets for our normal jackets. We start the GPS, click into our skis, tie the harnesses around our waists, and slide through the deep snow to the trail.

We had never camped in the winter or done a trip on skis before. "Move before you're ready" is our motto. We learn by doing and through our personal experiences. Here we wake up after a snowstorm in the wilderness between La Tabatière and Pakuashipi in Québec (opposite).

La Route Blanche is well-marked all the way from Kegashka to Blanc-Sablon. The snowmobile road is officially maintained and inspected by the government of Québec.

Comfort and discomfort in the snow

We follow a snowmobile trail along the north shore of the Saint Lawrence River. The sea lies to the south, and to the north, there is nothing but a vast white wilderness. The trail has the width of a normal road with signposts for villages, restaurants, and gas stations. Yet we hardly see any snowmobiles. Our only companions are the footprints of moose, wolves, hares, and squirrels. We are alone in a muted silence, intensely enjoying the peaceful white world. The only sound is the creaking of our skis and the rustling of our pants in rhythm with our movement. Every time we look at each other, we see big smiles and eyes filled with satisfaction. We have forgotten about last week's bad start.

Three days after Sept-Îles, we hardly see anyone on the trail. It is the last big town on the north shore and has less than 30,000 inhabitants. It is -20°C (4°F), cloudy, and there is a lot of wind. Today we ski with our jackets, hats, and thick gloves on. Suddenly, we hear the sound of snowmobiles. As always, we ski on the far right and move to the side as much as possible. The snowmobilers slow down, a big glove waves at us, and the helmet visor goes up.

"You guys are on the wrong trail," jokes the man on the first snowmobile. It's Norbert, our snowmobiler friend whom we met the day before we arrived in Sept-Îles when he surprised us with breakfast at our tent. "We have soup for you. You like that, right?"

Norbert says there's an old cabin farther down the trail. "We have brought a chainsaw. After the soup, we'll go to check the cabin and make sure there is enough firewood to survive the night." He taps his snowmobile, "Sit down, you've been standing all day. Seat heating." The carrot soup is delicious and the company heartwarming. He smiles as we contentedly enjoy the warm soup. *"C'est correct?"* he asks. It is more than fine, it's perfect.

After the short break, they drive to the cabin, and we ski on. Three hours later, they are on their way back and we get the rest of the soup. They tell us it is 9 more kilometers (5.6 miles). Just before dark, we find the cabin. It is a little crooked, but inside it is homey. Norbert has left two beers, bottles of water, tangerines, chocolates, and a hot meal on the table.

Skiing is not exhausting, but our days are long, and we suffer from minor aches and pains. Winter brings a range of new physical discomforts. Our elbows hurt from the force on ski poles, the sleds pull on our backs, we don't drink enough water, and our eyes burn from the cold wind. But it's the large blisters on Olivier's feet that concern us the most. Under normal circumstances, they would heal after a few days, but because of the cold, our feet are always covered. Letting his feet air out is not an option at -20°C (-4°F). In the morning, he squeezes his feet into his frozen boots rubbing open his blisters, which have barely had the chance to heal overnight. He has a painful grimace on his face for the first two hours on his skis until his feet get numb, and he can finally enjoy the day.

La Route Blanche

"Route Blanche" (White Trail) is written on the sign next to the trail. After more than a month, we finally reach the real goal of our skiing adventure. The asphalt road along the coast ends, and there is a missing link of over 400 kilometers (250 miles) to the continuation of the asphalt farther north. A rugged landscape of lakes, mountains, and marshlands makes it nearly impossible and very costly to connect the pieces of land. In an area as long as the Netherlands and Belgium combined, 4,000 people live in eight small fishing villages. By land, they are inaccessible from the outside world until winter arrives. Then all the lakes freeze over and form natural bridges. The brisk arctic cold and a layer of snow ensure that these residents can leave their village and taste freedom on their snowmobiles.

We stand at the gateway to the white road and prepare for a barren polar plain and extreme conditions. The white trail snakes out in front of us. Every 10 meters (33 feet) or so, there is a pole in the middle of a groomed track. Getting lost is impossible, and there are more than enough people passing by every day. The regularly spaced emergency shelters along the way are a luxury. Officially we are not supposed to sleep in them, but all the locals say we should. We consider the strong wind an emergency and take up residence in the second hut.

The hut is crooked, and the floor has not been swept in years. But after several days of wild camping, such a place feels like pure comfort. For us, this is much more than just four walls and a roof. There is a stove and a supply of firewood. When we come in, it is -10°C (14°F), but after an hour, the temperature is above freezing. The woodstove is not only practical, it also provides a relaxing atmosphere and a respite from the harsh elements. It allows us to easily melt snow, keep our food and shoes warm, and completely dry out our clothes and gear. Olivier is able to tape his blisters without freezing his toes, and the cozy warmth of the bench next to the stove provides pure comfort.

Our journey teaches us that enjoying the simple things in life like a warm fire is the greatest satisfaction we can have in the modern world. We have been living out of the same bags with the same set of clothes for almost four years. We own almost nothing but have everything we need. By stripping away all unnecessary possessions, we have learned to intensely enjoy simple things like a ray of sunshine that soothes the cold, a piece of chocolate before bed, or a crackling woodstove fire in a ramshackle hut. Being present for these simple and wonderful everyday moments is the key to true happiness.

Life on the edge

We feel at home in the simplicity of the north coast. Life is conducted at an obligatory slowness, caused by the seasons and the limited connections to the mainland. In winter, a small plane arrives once a week with fresh vegetables and dairy products. There are no cities, hospitals, or supermarkets. The luxury is silence, nature, and simplicity. It is a special culture that we hardly know in our busy modern lives. Life is traditional, at the mercy of circumstances, and almost entirely self-sufficient. In winter, working life is at a standstill. Most people rely on fishing which is only possible between April and October. The region flourished for a long time because of cod fishing, but overfishing has reduced the cod population considerably. These days, crabbing is the main industry.

One morning we pass Felix's garage. In front of the door is a large trap with a dead otter in it. Felix's daughter is petting the otter as if it was her stuffed animal and doesn't find the dead animal dirty or shocking. Inside, Felix is busy skinning a pine marten.

We are the only skiers on the trail, but there is plenty of snowmobile traffic. The snowmobilers always want to know why we are doing the trail on skis.

When we see him working, it seems like child's play. A short cut around the paws and then he peels off the entire skin. These are techniques we have never known, but here it is both tradition and a necessity of life. Children grow up with it. Self-sufficiency is a way of life and people build their own houses, can their own food, and fish for their winter stock in summer.

During our rest day in La Romaine, a small Innu First Nation Reserve, we are invited to go ice fishing. Zoë catches two river trout that we carry in our sled the next day and cook in the woodstove at an emergency shelter. While that dinner was luxurious, our lunch breaks are less relaxed on a long ski trip like this. It is too cold to sit still for more than 10 minutes. An hour before lunch, Zoë tucks a few tortillas under her jacket to thaw them out. We sprinkle grated Parmesan cheese on top, then chew on a handful of walnuts and that's our lunch. After two tortillas we are anything but full but are freezing cold. We ski on and are already looking forward to our next break and eating half-thawed energy bars that we put in our pockets in the morning.

The wind comes from behind most days, but on bad weather days, the icy blizzards blow right into our faces, biting at our skin. In Québec, we bought two face masks hoping they would protect our faces from frostbite—a constant concern in the extreme cold. Some days the windchill reaches -40°C (-40°F) and every spot of bare skin burns from the cold. The masks protect our faces and allow us to keep breathing, but we never imagined that they would serve a different purpose a few weeks later when the pandemic hit.

The zero-degree line is at sea level along the entire trail. Sometimes bays and stretches of the gulf freeze over, but in Magpie, Québec, there are now only loose pieces of ice floating in the water.

What is happiness

Every morning, we draw a card from a card game. They ask questions such as "What is the best gift you have ever had?" or "What is the best advice you have been given?" Today the question is, "Do you believe in true love?"

The mornings are cold, but once we're on our skis, our muscles warm up, we take off some layers of clothing, and our minds settle into a meditative state. We cross extensive lakes and glide rhythmically from pole to pole. As our arms and legs fall into opposite rhythms, our thoughts slowly float into their own world. It is a trance in which many discussions, questions, and feelings organically lead to meaningful insights throughout our journey.

Somewhere in the middle of the Pampa while cycling in Argentina, Zoë comes to a life-changing conclusion. "I'm happy!" she cries out of the blue. Awakened from her rhythmic trance, she rushes over to Olivier. "I didn't think I would ever say that I was happy. I thought happiness had to be perfect. There's always something to improve, and it can always be one step up, so how could I ever be happy?"

In the evening, we lie in our sleeping bags and Zoë wriggles over to Olivier. It's too cold to take our arms out of our sleeping bags, so Zoë puts her face against Olivier's.

"Honey, I only found out today that you are the one. Sometimes when I miss things, I dare not dream of our happiness. I thought you and our relationship weren't perfect enough, but nobody is perfect."

Olivier takes his arms out of the sleeping bag and pulls Zoë close to him. Zoë feels relieved. She has finally accepted that perfection does not exist. Not in happiness and not in a relationship. "You make me happy," she concludes.

"What was your childhood dream?" Zoë reads aloud. She puts the card back in the box and lifts her backpack. Yesterday's snowstorm has left the landscape under a white cloak. It is windless with a clear blue sky. Our nose hairs freeze together when we take deep breaths, but we feel intense happiness. Even after two months in the snow, the landscape still enchants us. There are few things that make us as happy as snow.

In the evening, we ski to the village of Harrington Harbour. The village is on an island surrounded by the ocean. We ski over frozen ice. The sun slowly sinks over the horizon as tiny flakes of snow swirl down. It is magical and we feel like the polar explorers of our childhood dreams.

As children, we both dreamed of being polar explorers. An impossible dream we always thought, but now we stand on enormous snowfields and feel like the polar explorers we dreamed of becoming.

Checkmate

It is barely eight days of skiing until the end of La Route Blanche. We are staying with a family in Saint-Augustin for the weekend. Zoë reconnects her phone to the internet. She opens the latest Facebook post where she praises the people of the Lower North Shore. She writes about our special encounters and thanks everyone for their unprecedented hospitality. Under the post are 150 comments. Virtually all of them are negative, aggressive, and personally directed.

"STAY AWAY from the Lower North Shore; you shouldn't be here; don't come to the small town of Old Fort; you are a danger to all of us; you will spread the virus; you will infect us; you are dumb and the people that host you even dumber; you are so selfish," and it goes in that vein.

A few days ago, the first signs of Covid-19 appeared in Canada. On the Lower North Coast, we are isolated from the world and safe. But suddenly there is a lot of fear in the area. With an elderly population and no hospitals, the virus could be fatal. Panic spreads faster than the virus.

For two months we were the heroes of the North Coast. Every day people stopped, curious about the two strange skiers. We felt honored. Everyone wanted to see us, meet us, and take a photo with us. In one single day, we are no longer those interesting skiers, but the infectious Europeans, the possible carriers of the virus, the scapegoats. We understand the fear but are upset by the negative reactions. Once again, one day changes our entire trip, just like the day in Ecuador when we heard that Zoë had a tumor on her ovaries. It is barely eight days until the end, but

that is eight too many. We have to end our skiing adventure and promptly leave the Lower North Shore.

We fly out on a small plane and are hosted by a nice family in a bigger town. The next two weeks are an emotional rollercoaster. We vacillate back and forth between staying in Canada and going back home. We are optimistic and think that the lockdown will be over in a few weeks, but after 10 days our host shatters that illusion. "I think it would be better for you to go home," he says at breakfast. "We want you to leave our house tomorrow."

For the second time in two weeks, we have to leave unexpectedly. We are in checkmate with a world that is locked down. That morning we feel nothing other than anger and negative feelings. We are angry with ourselves, with Covid, with our host, and with the whole situation. It seems heartbreaking, but the solution lies entirely within us. The only thing we can really control is our own attitude. Losing our good attitude is much worse than not achieving our goal.

We clear our heads. There is always a solution and always a positive side to every story. We didn't make it to the finish line, but we did live our impossible dream for two months. Covid is a setback, a very big one, but the whole world is suffering. It doesn't mean we have to end our journey, but we do need to take an obligatory pause, an unexpected detour. We arrive in Europe a month ahead of schedule, not by freighter but by plane.

When we land in the Netherlands, the weight falls off our shoulders. There is no anger anymore, just gratitude for the people of the North Coast. We were almost in checkmate, but the next move is up to us.

Felix releases a dead otter from a large trap (opposite). A sunny day with tailwinds makes for ideal conditions on La Route Blanche. Blizzards always come from the east with fierce headwinds (below).

Food, Water, and Snow
Keeping Well Fed and Hydrated

What is our calorie expenditure?

For a year and a half, Olivier kept track of his calorie expenditure with his sports watch. It distinguishes between active and passive calories. The passive calories are the energy the body uses at rest; the active calories are the energy we use during activities. On average we burned between 500 and 2,000 additional active calories on the days we were moving. This varied a little depending on the stage of our journey and how long our days were.

How did we replenish our calories?

It wasn't rocket science. If we burned 4,000 calories in a day, we needed to eat that amount. If we didn't, we might be okay for a few days, but eventually, we would burn out. More than just calories, vitamins, minerals, fiber, fats, and proteins are important for proper recovery. Our diet consisted mostly of carbohydrates such as oatmeal, bread, and pasta. Every evening meal we cooked with at least three different vegetables. We got protein from nuts, dairy products, and soy proteins. Fats we found in dairy products, peanut butter, nuts, and chocolate. We prefer the extra weight of fresh produce to an undernourished body. During the Appalachian Trail hike, we ate 3,000 calories per day, 500 calories too few on average. We both ended the hike much lighter than we started.

An example of our Appalachian Trail daily diet (per person)

- Breakfast: 100 grams (3.5 ounces) of oatmeal, powdered milk, 30 grams (1 ounce) of granola, a handful of nuts and raisins, and sometimes fresh fruit—600 calories
- Lunch: Bread, bagels, or wraps with cheese, avocado, walnuts, or peanut butter— 800 calories
- Snacks: Trail mix (nuts, chocolate, and dried fruit), energy bars, and bananas—500 calories
- Dinner: 200 grams (7 ounces) of pasta with sour cream and at least three vegetables—1,000 calories
- Dessert: A piece of chocolate, some chips, or a cookie—100 calories

When there was more food available, we took full advantage of it. We stuffed ourselves with fruit and carbohydrates in villages. We carried fresh food in a lightweight thermal bag, similar to a freezer bag from the supermarket. We always carried an emergency meal.

We applied a similar approach on other parts of our journey when there wasn't the security of regular villages to top off our food. In remote areas like Québec, we had to prepare meals in advance and mail them ahead to various locations along our route.

Drinking water

The only time we got sick from water was when we stayed with a family in Huánuco, Peru. The house looked upscale, and without thinking, Zoë turned on the tap, filled a glass, and drank it. She was sprinting to the toilet every half hour for the next three days.

How did we find safe drinking water?

We have learned that for many people in the world, accessing water is not as simple as turning on the tap. In Africa and large parts of South America, taps were shut off to save water and the water that did come out wasn't drinkable. People often had to walk miles to a well. Wherever we were in the world, we went through the same process to find safe drinking water:

- Ask. Our preference was always to ask for water. It was a simple way to connect with people and practice the language. Depending on the country, water came from a tap, a bottle, or a large barrel of spring or rainwater.
- Nature. We often drank water from nature. Especially while hiking, canoeing, and skiing when we were far from civilization.
- Buying water. We preferred not to buy bottled water. It creates plastic waste and a lot of CO_2 emissions.

Our main water rules

- We always asked the locals if they drank the water. If they drank it or boiled it first, so did we.
- We drank unfiltered water from rivers and lakes where there was no run-off from agriculture, houses, or mining. We never drank stagnant water.
- If we were unsure, we boiled or filtered the water. A good filter will remove bacteria, protozoa, and most viruses, but boiling is the safest option. Be sure to boil it for at least three minutes.

On average, we only filtered or boiled our water one out of every 10 times. So, most water was safe to drink, as long as we followed our main rules. In Huánuco, we forgot our rules for one moment. It turned out the water from the fancy tap came from a spring surrounded by mining.

How much water did we carry?

The amount of water we needed per day varied according to our mode of transportation and the season. Below is a list of the amount of water we carried and the containers we used. Whenever possible, we saved the water we carried for drinking only. We used local sources for showering, washing dishes, and cooking as much as we could.

- Bicycle: 4 liters (1 gallon):
  2 × water bottle 0.75 L + PET bottle 1.5 L + Nalgene bottle 1 L
- Canoe: 6 liters (1.5 gallons):
  2 × Nalgene bottle 1 L + water sack 4 L
- Hiking: 3.25 liters (0.85 gallon):
  1 × water bottle 0.75 L + PET bottle 1.5 L + Nalgene bottle 1 L
- Skating: 9 liters (2.4 gallons):
  2 × camel bag 2L + water sack 4 L + Nalgene bottle 1 L
- Skiing: 4.5 liters (1.2 gallons):
  thermo bottle 1.5 L + 2 × thermo bottle 1L + Nalgene bottle 1 L

*PET bottle = Polyethylene terephthalate plastic bottles, or the kind that are used for bottled water and soda. We reused the ones we found discarded.

Surviving in the snow

To survive the cold, we learned to act counterintuitively:

- Swinging our arms and moving our hands to encourage blood flow to the extremities despite the urge to pull them into our body warmth.
- Keeping on the move to generate body heat even when we felt like resting.
- Getting out of the tent to pee when we would rather stay in our warm sleeping bags meant less energy was wasted keeping the pee inside of us warm, and it let us get back to sleep quickly.
- Changing into thermal underwear after skiing despite not feeling like it meant we slept better in our warm, dry clothes.
- Taking off our down jackets before skiing when we were still cold was unpleasant, but it prevented us from sweating and making our other layers damp.
- Putting our down jackets back on when we stopped even though we were warm, meant that we retained our body heat.

BACK ON THE ROAD

Roller-Skiing from the Netherlands to Sweden

On the face of it, even we have to admit that the idea of roller-skiing is quite absurd. We explain our plans, and we are almost universally met with concern. We don't have that many worries ourselves. Traveling by human power has become second nature to us like a comfort zone. The only change has been the mode of transportation. A new sport brings new questions. Can we handle it physically? Can we skate on any surface? How many kilometers can we cover each day? But, we have asked those kinds of questions many times over now. The unknowns remain unknown until we start. We will adapt and thrive.

The first meters on roller skis are particularly tough. Fortunately, the Netherlands is as flat as a pancake with bike paths everywhere—perfect for getting used to our new mode of transportation. Our roller skis have inflatable tires that allow us to skate on unpaved surfaces.

Our New Sport

The Journey Is the Training

It only took that one afternoon in Fort Kent, for us to impulsively decide that roller-skiing would be our new way of traveling. Roller skis are long skates—or skis with skate wheels on the base if you prefer—and the technique to use them is a combination of the two sports too. We use ski poles with sharp steel tips that grip the road to provide extra propulsion. We combine that with an almost side-to-side skating motion. It is easier said than done. Now that we have the skates on our feet again, we feel like beginners. They feel awkward and our ankles wobble in all directions. Olivier especially curses the poles which seem better at getting away from him than anything else. We contemplate changing our plans, but we have the time to practice, and Olivier devises a training plan. Technique drills build both our skills and confidence.

Zoë's devises a braking system for our trailers with a handle at hip height. It is not perfect because to brake, we have to take one ski pole out of our hand, but it's functional and safe. The only question is whether the brakes will work on downhills. Because there aren't many hills in the Netherlands, we don't have the chance to really put our braking system to the test before forging out.

It's early June, and European borders are opening again. We have a plan; we will roller-ski to Sweden. We don't miss a beat and leave as soon as possible.

At 9:30 a.m., Zoë's parents wave goodbye to us from their front door. We are geared up with skates underfoot, hip belts fastened, poles in hand, helmets on our heads, and loaded-down trailers behind us. Compared to hauling our sleds when skiing, our trailers seem almost empty. But with our food supplies for the first few days, we are still lugging 35 kilos (77 pounds) each. We stumble and bounce over the cobblestones of Breda.

As we pass through the city, people stop walking, construction workers put down their tools, and delivery men forget their packages for a moment. Roller skis are virtually unknown to the Dutch, and our self-made trailer construction is also a novelty. We, for the most part, are too busy concentrating to notice, dodging bumps in the road and trying to control our wayward poles. Just outside the city, we cross the freeway over a small bridge. Puffing, we lean on our poles for a rest when we reach the top.

"My god, I don't know if we'll make it," Zoë says.

"My heart rate is at 180," pants Olivier, who is dripping with sweat.

In the evening, we plop down in the grass. We have been skating over 40 kilometers (25 miles) in the flat Netherlands. There wasn't a breath of wind, and the highest mountain was the bridge over the freeway. Olivier's watch indicates five hours of intensive sport with over 5,000 calories burned—more than a marathon.

"Two more marathons, and then we'll have skate legs," Olivier says after a refreshing dip in the river. His face is still red from the exercise. "We'll be fit in a few weeks," he says, smiling.

On the way to the promised land

We hardly know the east side of the Netherlands. Although a lot is recognizable, it also feels like we are exploring. We see thatched roofs and people wearing clogs, hear different accents, and pass through places with names that sound more German than Dutch.

Our bodies are finally starting to get used to our new sport. We can look around and enjoy the scenery, our average heart rate is a lot lower, and we are not so exhausted at every break. After 10 days, we cross the border into Germany. No fences, no police, no inspections, no barriers, and no stamps in our passports. Unfortunately, also no "Welcome to Germany" sign, but that's not necessary. One difference is immediately apparent. The beautiful Dutch bike path turns into a long road of uneven cobblestones. We have already categorized our favorite surfaces. There are countless types of asphalt, but they all roll well. Uphill is tough, but our technique to deal with that is getting better. On the first short descents, our brakes were fine. Cobblestones, however, well, they are *Scheiße* as the Germans would say.

Northern Germany is not that different from the Netherlands. We see the same types of thatched roofs, cowsheds, dikes, and grassy fields. The strong winds and daily rains blow us through Germany, and before we know it, we are at the doorstep of Denmark. Scandinavia, at last—the "promised land." Although we have never been there, the pictures of the region have always enchanted us. We dream of living in Scandinavia and perhaps even settling down there. Denmark is just a warm-up; Norway and Sweden are our real goals. After permission from the Danish police, we slip between the large sandbags that barricade the Danish border and stand in country number 24. The grassy meadows turn into undulating fields of grain and the dairy industry into pigsties with tiny windows. We don't understand the people, and the road signs have letters we don't know how to pronounce. The first few days all the people say "*Bonjour*" and "*Bon route.*"

"They all think I have the French flag," Zoë keeps saying. A few days later we realize that they were actually shouting "*God tur,*" have a nice trip.

Rest

Since the very first day of our trip, we have been battling an inner struggle. We have a yearning to keep moving forward and maintain momentum, but also a fear that we will simply let the journey pass by, and the act of traveling will overwhelm everything else we seek to experience.

It's in our Western genes to compartmentalize our lives as much as possible. The unexpected return from Colombia taught us a very important lesson about being present. In one day, we returned from the laid-back "*mañana-mañana*" culture of South America to the overly scheduled, busy pace of the Netherlands.

"We are back home! Can we come over tomorrow?" Zoë asks a friend.

"Oops, I can't tomorrow, but next Thursday at 8 p.m., I have time."

It's the culture that's in our genes too; the one we grew up with. Even when traveling, we are constantly planning, thinking ahead, and considering the next day. We are champions of filling all our time, even when we have nothing to do. Efficiency we call it, but is it really effective? Aren't we forgetting something very important like fully living in the present moment?

At 2 a.m., our ferry reaches Norway. We are tingling with excitement and curiosity as we begin to explore our possible new home country. What do the houses look like, are there bicycle paths, do they have normal bread, and do the people say a friendly hello? We are already thinking about the future, but that future

Per and Birte check the honey production of their bees at their holiday home on the east coast of the Jutland region (opposite). The weather is rainy and windy when we arrive on the island of Mors in Denmark (above).

The Netherlands and Northern Germany are mostly flat. In Denmark, the first hills start, but it is still just a warm-up for the mountains of Norway.

will only come later. We remind ourselves of an agreement we had made before we left on skates. "In Scandinavia, we're going to make more time for camping and enjoying nature," Zoë said.

Zoë has two bushcraft books to learn from in her trailer. Olivier, too, increasingly craves out moments without the internet and to-do lists. Yet it remains a difficult task for us to consciously choose to slow down.

In the evening we find a beautiful spot by a lake. "Let's stay here for a day?" Olivier proposes.

"A rest day here? Aren't you going to be bored?" asks Zoë, surprised.

"Some hiking, reading a book, and enjoying this beautiful place. One day I will master it," says Olivier.

Life on the road

- Routine is part of life, and there is nothing wrong with it. It provides the structure and efficiency that helps us to achieve our goals and dreams. But routine should not become a rut. By breaking away from time to time and letting the unknown run its course, we continue to live a surprising and adventurous life.
- Living outside is an adventure and not always easy, but through discipline and routine, we make it as enjoyable as possible.
- Being rich isn't about having more, it's about being happy with less.
- Happiness doesn't come from what we have. It's a choice and an attitude.
- Time is our most valuable possession.

In Norway and Sweden, they have *allemannsretten*—the freedom to roam on uncultivated land. This means that everybody who travels by nonmotorized transportation has the right to camp, bathe, rest, fish, and forage on public or privately owned land and water.

When we are in Hamar, Norway, a local man tells us that we can see reindeer in Femundsmarka National Park. We change our route and skate 250 kilometers (155 miles) north. The reindeer are semiwild, herded by the Sami.

Rule number ten

We skate along a bad gravel road that looked a lot better on Google Street View. We bounce our way over loose stones. We are well past the halfway mark of our distance for the day, and Olivier's stomach is rumbling. Suddenly, a motorcyclist comes out of the field and rides over to us.

Farmer Jan-Tore sits bare-chested on his motorcycle and looks at our skates with admiration. "We have a beach by the lake. Do you want to come for a swim?" he asks.

Zoë initially declines the offer thinking about our plans down the road, but Olivier surprises her by gratefully accepting. He is ready for a lunch break and knows we can make up the time later if they want. Pleased, Jan-Tore invites us to follow him to the red farmhouse overlooking a beautiful lake. At the water's edge, there is a large party tent. Next to it are two kayaks and a jetty with a motorboat and diving board.

"The water is nice and warm," Jan-Tore assures us. It is a beautiful summer day of about 25°C (77°F) with no wind. "If you want to stay a night, you can pitch your tent here," he suggests and hands us apple pie and sodas. The further north, the colder the people, we sometimes hear, but hospitality knows no bounds. In cold countries, people also have warm hearts.

At night in the tent, we open our notebook on the page "household rules WeLeaf." It is difficult for us to suddenly change our plans. We are often too competitive in reaching our daily goal and find it hard to be satisfied with half a day of exercise. After four years of traveling, we add a final rule to our list: never decline an invitation.

The Telemark region is sometimes called "little Norway" because it has everything Norway has to offer (above). The orange dot next to the water is our tent on Jan-Tore's farm (opposite).

For the last 200 kilometers (124 miles) on skates, we follow the Klarälven River (top). Sweden has hundreds of free cabins and shelters, such as this pilgrim's chapel near Mora, where everyone can enjoy the *friluftsliv*—open-air life (bottom).

Open-Air Life

Scandinavia as Our Home Away from Home

Zoë's hair is washed and wet. The water in the lake is barely 15°C (60°F), but the dip feels like a release. There is nothing more refreshing than a cold dip after several long days of sports. She scrubs her sports shirt over a stone. When all eight garments are washed, Olivier wrings them out and hangs them over the clothesline slung between two trees. The wind and sun do the rest. Next to it is our temporary home, a beautiful wooden shelter, within which we have set up our tent. The shelter has three walls and is open at the front; it is more than we need. We have just arrived and already feel completely at home.

We entered Sweden three days ago and the steep climbs around the Norwegian fjords immediately gave way to a more rolling landscape, with even more forests and lakes. We have been sleeping in the tent for 15 nights in a row, but the Swedes aren't surprised by that. We meet people everywhere in nature being active. People fish, hike, or forage berries and mushrooms in the forest. Yesterday, we saw a family picnicking in the rain, and earlier, we saw people taking a morning swim in the cold lakes. Regularly, we see families grilling over campfires. It makes us happy. The Scandinavian people show us that it is possible to combine a love for the outdoors with everyday life. They all balance the responsibilities of jobs, houses, and families, yet they make enjoying the great outdoors a priority. *Friluftsliv*—open-air life—they call it.

In the forest, we collect dry wood for our campfire. Making the campfire is Zoë's job. Disciplined, she arranges the twigs in piles from thin to thick. This is how she learned it, and this is how she always succeeds. Olivier rinses the sand from the freshly picked chanterelles and fills a pan with water from the lake. The kitchen is his territory and his moment of rest after a day on the skates. The main course is pasta with cream, onions, and mushrooms. A loaf of bread is slowly baking in our collapsible oven next to the fire. It is our dessert, along with the blueberries we receive from nature every day. We sit on the bench around the fire pit and watch the dancing flames. It's not cold, but still, we sit close together. The only sound is the crackling of the pine. The water is a perfect mirror, and the first stars twinkle gently in the sky.

Our childhood home will always be our home, but the outdoors is our home away from home. The outdoors are always near in Scandinavia. They are in the air and in the people. During the day we count the miles, but these evenings are what really make us enjoy life.

The last day

The skate plan that we made in Fort Kent was to board a freighter ship in Canada and sail to Germany. From there, we would skate through Scandinavia and then end in the Netherlands. Thus, the circle would be complete. Covid meant the circle would not be complete but gave us the freedom to leave for Scandinavia with no final destination. Fate would decide.

In the middle of September, we receive a message from Walter, a colleague of Olivier's father's who has been following our journey since the start. He has an offer to make. "Our vacation home in Sweden is vacant so you can spend the winter there," Walter writes. We look at the map, see that we passed that region two weeks ago, turn around, and skate via a detour to our new destination.

"Last day," Olivier whispers as he gently wakes Zoë. The rain patters quietly on the tent. A tractor hums in the meadow, and an occasional car drives on the asphalt road in the distance. We have woken up to these sounds in the background so many times. The walls of the tent visibly separate us from what is out there, but we can hear, feel, and smell it. In an hour, the tent will be packed up, but for now, we enjoy the last morning in our portable home.

15 kilometers (9.3 miles) remain to our final destination. A walk to the front door and back compared to our total travel distance. A few weeks ago, we completed 40,000 kilometers (25,000 miles) via human power, equal to the circumference of the earth.

"It takes so long to get there," people often say when they see us traveling. That's the idea. We want to travel slowly, to see and smell the environment, to notice details of the culture, and to work our muscles. We don't choose the fast lane but the path of adventure. There is no better way to discover a country than to travel through it slowly.

We cover the last few meters on foot. We don't do that to extend our last day, but out of necessity. Two days ago, a crack appeared in Olivier's skate, so we have been half walking, half tentatively sliding to the finish. No cruising, just hard work. That's how we like it and secretly we think it has to end this way.

Then suddenly we are in the driveway of the vacation home. We have lived on the road for four years, but our life underway ends here. It was exactly four years ago on the 30th of September, 2016 that we got on our bikes in Amsterdam at the beginning of our trip. It felt perfectly normal, a day like any other.

The circle is now complete, but that was never the main objective. It just worked out that way, just like everything else along our journey. Today also feels perfectly normal, a day like any other. The 1,459 days before made our journey, not this single one.

Our journey using human propulsion allowed us to discover unknown roads, meet amazing people, and explore remote villages. It kept us moving and put our minds at ease. Our bikes, legs, canoe, skis, and roller skis allowed us to go places most tourists never go and opened up a new world for us as travelers. It was a life experienced outside, with many active hours a day at the mercy of the elements. It exercised our ingenuity in keeping ourselves warm and fed, washing dishes without water, and finding places to sleep. We lived a life where we were at peak fitness, lived in two sets of clothes, enjoyed jumping into cold water, and called 10 drops of water a bath. It was a life where we challenged our bodies, instead of living inside our minds.

Throughout our journey, we tried our best to travel sustainably. It cost almost nothing, but it gave us so much in return. Physically, we pushed our limits, and mentally, we achieved peace. We focused decisively on one goal at a time, followed by immense satisfaction when we reached it. We developed ourselves, became a strong team, and found answers to personal questions. We discovered the culture of different countries and saw a world that was much better than the media had portrayed. We learned about generosity, the value of family and friends, living in the now, and being happy with what we have. Our luxury was living out our dream.

The people we meet

- Everywhere we go, we look for a balance between being a guest and feeling at home.
- Generosity knows no boundaries. The world is full of good people with big hearts.
- Hospitality is synergistic. People give, and we give back. The most beautiful quality of receiving hospitality is that we want to pay it back.
- To understand and communicate in other cultures, we must learn to look through the other person's lens. Our frame of reference is not the only correct one.
- Prejudices make our world smaller. They are learned, but fortunately, we can unlearn them.

The sky clears after a heavy rain. We have learned to live with the elements and enjoy the little things, like the sun coming back out. Mostly, it's the little things that put smiles on our faces.

Our Self-Care Rituals

How to Keep Clean and Motivated

Daily hygiene

Hygiene is incredibly important for our mental and physical state. Being clean helped us to feel fresh mentally and—just as important-ly—avoid physical sickness and injuries like chaffing or saddle sores. We, therefore, aimed to wash every single day.

There were times when water was scarce, like in the Chaco. Combined with the heady heat, it was one of the many reasons cycling there was so challenging. Despite the scarcity of water, there wasn't a day that we skipped our wash. Even if some of our "baths" were unconventional like washing from a bucket of brown water while a bunch of schoolchildren watched curiously.

On the Appalachian Trail, we hiked with Gary. We met him when he arrived at the camp-ground, panting. Drops of sweat were running down his face. He set up his tent and plopped down, exhausted, in his wet clothes. We hiked together for several days. Unfortunately, he had to drop out to give his chaffed skin a rest.

Everywhere his backpack touched his body, his skin was rubbed raw by the dry sweat on his skin. Gary's misfortune reinforced the idea that dry clothes and a clean body are of utmost importance in staying healthy.

Where did we wash?

- Natural water sources: Ideally, we would jump into a river or lake, but often we had to be happy with a small spring or stream. We took a bottle and used it to pour water over ourselves.
- Water bottles: We didn't have a large water capacity to shower extensively. With a washcloth and five drops for each body part, we removed the sweat and grime of the day. Sometimes we would take an extra PET bottle (found everywhere along the street, unfortunately) and two caps. In one cap we poked holes to create a makeshift shower. Later in the trip, we added a four-liter water sack which we also used for bathing.
- Showers: In people's homes and in hostels we could shower.

- Spigots or garden hoses: near gardens, churches, and soccer fields we often found spigots or garden hoses. If no one was around, we bathed underneath.

Other practicalities

- We never used soap when in nature; not when washing dishes, showering, or washing our hands. It is bad for the environment and not necessary.
- Zoë had an IUD, which meant she had very light and short periods. She just needed one panty liner per day. For future trips, she wants to try washable panty liners.
- We had two pairs of socks and three pairs of underwear for hiking, canoeing, skiing, and skating. For the evening, we had one pair of "clean" socks and underwear that we used several days in a row.
- We used a single pair of cycling shorts each. We washed them once a week, as with the rest of our clothes if there was an opportunity. We rinsed them more frequently when possible.

Tips for motivation

- Remember that there is always a reward to any endeavor—a fresh shower, sunshine, views, wildlife. Any pain you are experiencing will soon be forgotten, but the memories of the rewards will endure.
- Use positive language with yourself. "I want to do this," and "I am going to finish this."
- Take care of your body: maintain personal hygiene, eat healthily, and get enough sleep.
- Focus on taking small steps. Look at the challenge of the day, not the 1,000 kilometers ahead.

- The more routines you have, the more mental energy you will have left to achieve your goals.
- Don't ignore homesickness. It is an important signal from your body.
- Give yourself time to think about what you miss: adventure, love, home, or structure.
- Do something different to gain new impetus and energy.
- Move before you are ready. Moving physically helps to avoid over-researching or overthinking.

How do we make choices?

- Recognize that you have a choice to make and hit the start button.
- Choose a time limit, for example, "ten minutes" or "when we get to that curve."
- Think about the choice individually. If it is an important choice, it helps to write down all the arguments separately. Discuss the individual choices.
- There is a strong possibility that you have come to the same decision. If not, you have clear arguments to make a good decision together

Budget, Spending, and Personal Records

How We Saved, What We Spent, and Our Lifestyle on the Road

"Are you billionaires?" was the most frequently asked question during our trip. We saved up with the idea of being able to travel indefinitely and independently. In our minds "indefinitely" meant three years, and we wanted to have some savings left over when we returned.

Anticipated budget for two people
€30 ($32) a day
Planned budget per year: €11,000 ($12,000)
Total savings target: €50,000 ($54,000)

We saved €1,000 ($1,100) per month over four years in anticipation of our trip. We had a cheap rental house and didn't buy any luxury items. We used a small part of our budget before starting our trip. The second-hand bikes, outdoor gear, and clothing cost us about €4,000 ($4,300) to which family, friends, and colleagues contributed a major part.

How much did we spend?
Our actual daily budget after four years of travel averaged €18.40 ($19.80) a day for both of us. That was about €550 ($590) per month or €6,700 ($7,200) per year. The total cost for our four-year journey was €23,410 ($25,145).

By far, we spent the most money on food. The rest we spent on overnight stays, spare parts, public transportation, tourist attractions, souvenirs, SIM cards, and visas.

Did we live like vagrants?
18 euros a day sounds like an impossibly low amount, but in reality, it allowed us to:
· Eat healthy and varied food every day
· Occasionally eat in a restaurant and buy croissants at the bakery
· Sleep in hostels every now and then
· Buy spare parts
· Pay for buses and ferries
· Fly home in case of emergency
· Visit national parks and museums
· Take the occasional tourist tour
· Buy new clothes or camping gear when something was worn out
· Keep our website online

How was this possible in the U.S. and Scandinavia?
We actually ended up spending the least amount of money in Norway. The U.S. was in third place in terms of spending, and Sweden was in fifth place. In Peru and Bolivia, we could eat lunch for barely one and a half euros or sleep in a cheap hotel for five euros, so we took full advantage of that. On the other hand, the cheapest hotel in the U.S. cost about €55 ($60) a night, so we didn't sleep in hotels or eat in restaurants there. The result was that the most expensive countries were actually the cheapest afterward because we avoided spending money in them.

Did we have income?
We made a conscious decision to save before the trip, so we didn't need to earn money while traveling. Documenting our trip was our "work," which was almost a full-time job, but we didn't make any immediate money from our website, Instagram, or YouTube channels.

We received a small amount of income during our trip from family, friends, colleagues, and people we met on our journey who contributed to our travels. For the last two years, we worked with outdoor companies and received merchandise in exchange for advertising and testing.

Good Samaritans
We knew that 30 euros a day would allow us to travel completely independently. However, we never expected to be helped so much along the way. There were countless people who invited us into their homes, gave us food, surprised us with hotel stays, took us to restaurants, or paid for our groceries. We are extremely grateful to the countless generous people we have met on our journey.

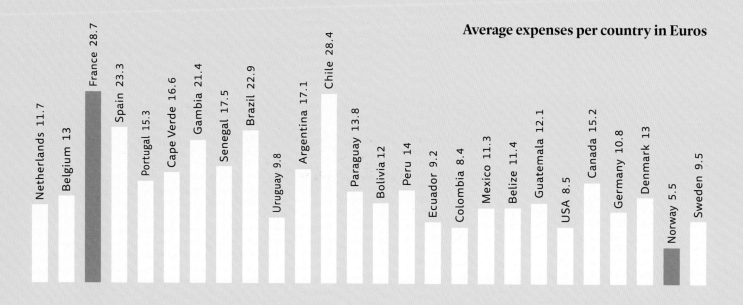

Average expenses per country in Euros

Netherlands 11.7 · Belgium 13 · France 28.7 · Spain 23.3 · Portugal 15.3 · Cape Verde 16.6 · Gambia 21.4 · Senegal 17.5 · Brazil 22.9 · Uruguay 9.8 · Argentina 17.1 · Chile 28.4 · Paraguay 13.8 · Bolivia 12 · Peru 14 · Ecuador 9.2 · Colombia 8.4 · Mexico 11.3 · Belize 11.4 · Guatemala 12.1 · USA 8.5 · Canada 15.2 · Germany 10.8 · Denmark 13 · Norway 5.5 · Sweden 9.5

Punctures

The first 4,000 kilometers (2,485 miles) in Europe brought us seven flat tires. Olivier was "winning" with six to one. After 500 kilometers (310 miles) in Brazil, our number doubled. Olivier still led, but Zoë was quickly catching up: nine to five to Olivier. It was thanks to a combination of our own ignorance and the circumstances. We had no idea that the quality of the bicycle tire made such a big difference. Only a few months later, we replaced the cheap Brazilian and Argentinian tires with Schwalbe anti-puncture tires in Mendoza, Argentina. The 4,000 kilometers (2,485 miles) from Mendoza to Ushuaia, over roads much worse than Brazil, resulted in only one flat tire for each of us. Flat tire competition final score:
Olivier 18 to Zoë 15

What did we have to replace during our journey?

Clothes
- 3 pairs of shoes Olivier
- 2 pairs of shoes Zoë
- 2 pairs of Birkenstocks
- 2 pairs of shorts
- 1 pair of leggings
- 2 t-shirts
- 2 pairs of cycling shorts
- 2 jackets
- 1 windbreaker
- 2 pairs of sunglasses
- 2 pairs of gloves
- At least 10 pairs of socks and underwear

The bike
- 4 × rims (because of the rim brakes)
- 2 × wheel hubs
- 13 × tires
- 2 × mudguards
- 2 × cassettes
- 2 × chain rings
- 4 × chains
- 3 × gear cables
- 4 × brake cables
- Dozens of inner tubes and brake pads
- 3 × saddles
- 2 × spokes
- 3 × drinking bottles
- 1 × mirror
- 2 × pedals
- 1 × gear shifter

Other things that wore out
- 3 sleeping bag liners
- 1 daypack
- 2 sleeping bags
- 4 inflatable mats
- 1 fuel stove
- 2 ponchos
- 1 phone
- 2 ski poles

Lost gear
- 1 pair of pants
- 2 towels
- 4 spatulas
- 1 seat pad

Personal records

- Highest speed:
  77.6 kilometers (48.2 miles) per hour in Guatemala
- Longest daily distance:
  146.7 kilometers (91.1 miles) in Mexico
- Highest bike average:
  29 kilometers (18 miles) per hour
- Slowest bike average:
  4.6 kilometers (2.8 miles) per hour in Guatemala
- Cycling without rest days:
  11 days
- Times 100+ kilometers (62+ miles):
  52 days
- Highest point:
  4,878 meters (16,004 feet) in Peru
- Highest camping spot:
  4,256 meters (13,936 feet) in Peru
- Days without showers:
  4 weeks (sailing)
- Most food carried:
  14 days' worth (canoeing, skiing)
- Strongest wind:
  150 kilometers (93 miles) per hour in Argentina
- Highest temperature:
  48 °C (118 °F) in Senegal
- Lowest temperature:
  -35 °C (-31 °F) in Canada
- Nights in a row in our tent:
  19 in Scandinavia
- Most elevation gain in one day:
  2,421 meters (7,943 feet) in Peru
- Longest day on human power:
  12 hours and 20 minutes on the Appalachian Trail

Average time on the move per day per sport

🚲 Cycling 4h10

🥾 Hiking 5h20

🛶 Canoeing 6h10

🎿 Skiing 5h50

⛸ Skating 4h00

Av. time on the move from A to B 8h00

Sharing our journey with others

We like to share our stories and adventures and knew we would keep a blog, but our approach evolved while we traveled.

- Blog: we wrote a story every two weeks or so, on average
- Social media: we posted pictures on Instagram and Facebook several times a week
- Videos: we filmed a lot during the trip, and it took us a long time to work out how best to share the footage. After Mexico, we started editing long episodes together. We published our videos via YouTube.
- Map: we kept track of our exact route and every place we slept on an interactive map with Google *My Maps*.
- Sports achievements: we shared our daily sports achievements on Strava, including a short story.
- Excel: we collected data about our journey as we went.

What was in our electronics bag?

We lugged around a whole bag full of camera gear so that we could fully capture our journey. In total, our equipment weighed almost 10 kilos (22 pounds).

- Nikon D3300 including five batteries
- Two lenses: 18–110 and 50 millimeter
- A camera timer, microphone, and aluminum tripod
- XStorm 15,000 mAh power bank
- GoPro including two batteries
- Mavic Air drone with three batteries
- A laptop and an external hard drive

How much work was it?

Capturing our trip was a lot of work, but all the memories we now hold made it worth it. We photographed and filmed almost every day. Some days we stopped as many as 20 times. Sometimes this was just for a quick snap, sometimes we set up the tripod. On average, we probably spent an hour a day shooting and filming.

We would write in the tent or during rest days, just using our phones or laptop. Each blog post took around four hours to write, including translating it into English. We edited photos and videos on our laptop with Adobe Lightroom and Final Cut Pro respectively. Photo editing was a fairly quick process, but a YouTube episode often took 50 hours. As time went on, we needed to dedicate more and more time to answering the messages and questions we got via social media. We often get asked how much we earned from all this. The answer is nothing, other than the chance to share our story and the energy it gives us when we hear we have inspired someone.

Our ten rules

Our rules and habits give us footing, confidence, and direction when making choices.

1. We never cycle in the dark.
2. We never cycle on highways (unless there is no other option).
3. We always carry an emergency meal in our packs.
4. We eat everything we are offered, even if the food is something we normally wouldn't eat.
5. We make camp no later than one and a half hours before dark.
6. We always ask if the water is drinkable unless we are really sure.
7. We try to do more than half of the day's distance before lunch.
8. We wash ourselves and change into clean clothes at the end of each day.
9. We heed warnings of "here it is dangerous" (but take warnings of "there it is dangerous" with a pinch of salt)
10. We never decline an invitation.

Epilogue

"What are you going to do after the trip?" We've been asked that a lot since finishing our journey.

Sitting in the cabin in Sweden, we lay out a literal blank page in front of us. We fill it with our dreams of a simple life full of adventure and new journeys with lots of time for friends and family. We envision ourselves in a small house surrounded by nature and countless opportunities to exercise in the great outdoors.

We dream. The journey has taught us never to hold back our dreams. If we want something in our lives, we have to give it our all. It's not easy, but it's not impossible either. A dream is nothing more than a different turn in life. Adventures take us beyond the known paths, but they can also bring new fears and uncertainties. Our biggest concern is whether we will ever get used to the routine of society again. Did the world trip do us any good, or did it just leave us with an insatiable desire for more?

We realize that our choices are in our own hands. Our journey has given us the tools to make decisions and the confidence that we will make the best of the result. We have learned that life is long enough to make mistakes but too short to worry about them. We know that our preferences will change, and that above all, we should enjoy the life we are living right now. The journey has given us a positive outlook. We have learned to turn our fears into new challenges.

We have become different people over the last four years. Zoë has learned to control her temper, turn jealousy into pride, recognize the limits of perfectionism, admit when she is wrong, and say thank you. Olivier has found his social side, a willingness to give up some control and enjoy spontaneity.

His giving muscle has developed, and he can actually enjoy doing nothing. As a couple, we now look at life differently. We are less materialistic and less career-oriented. Family, simplicity, time, and friendship are now our top priorities. We see the goodness and generosity that lies within each person. We look at the environment with concern and adjust our lifestyles accordingly. We cook without meat and have changed our bank accounts to sustainable banks. We have begun to realize that balance is the answer to many questions—a simple vision that calls for not too much and not too little.

Our next adventure is not a physical challenge of 40,000 kilometers (25,000 miles) but a tactical one of trying to settle in Scandinavia. It is just as exciting, just as new, and just as adventurous as the previous one. An adventurous life is one with a take-charge attitude toward changing our lives and trying new things that we find exciting or make us curious. We hope this book gives you the tools and confidence to live adventurously whatever your adventure might be: learning to play the piano, starting to read, learning a new language, or camping with your grandchildren. If you really want something, anything is possible, but the hardest part of any endeavor is taking the first step. There is only one way, and that is to just do it. Our world trip didn't fill our blank pages, but it did give us all the qualities and confidence to write them. In doing so, we have learned that there is seemingly no end to where human power can take us.

With much love,
Zoë and Olivier

Acknowledgments

Over the past four years, hundreds of people have asked us, "Are you going to write a book?" All these people have unconsciously planted a small seed in our minds that eventually became this book. For us, this book is a privileged opportunity to share how we learned what is possible without having experience, and what the reward is for doing things ourselves. Without the hundreds of people who have helped along our journey, joined us for a section, or provided warm meals and shelter, we would have never learned as much and the journey would never have lasted so long. You have always been our inspiration to travel, to keep going, and to write our story.

In October 2021, the Dutch version of our book, *Op Eigen Kracht,* was released—a dream come true. Our book is our life's work, something we wrote, designed, and created ourselves with the help of some amazing people. Right from the beginning, we wanted to make the book available in English. We translated our work and sent it out to various publishers, but actually had only one publishing house in mind: gestalten. Their work has inspired us for a long time, and we dreamed about having our story transformed into a book together with them. In October 2022, our new dream became a reality, and our persistence was rewarded with success. We thank Robert Klanten for having confidence in our story from the moment we pitched our book. And we thank the entire team at gestalten for creating another piece of art in their collection. Because of you, we continue to share our inspiration.

The translation of our book wouldn't have been possible without the help of our dear friends and outdoor enthusiasts: Pat Theriault and Paul Kile from Fort Kent, Maine. Next, Tom Hill did an incredible job editing the English text and preserving the power of our story. Finally, we want to thank Janneke Klop for introducing us to her contacts within the gestalten team.

After our world trip, our journey continued. We fell in love with Scandinavia and decided that we wanted to make our basecamp there. We currently reside in Norway where we continue our adventurous lifestyle. We practice what we preach and challenge everyone to incorporate some adventure into their lives. We organize human-powered adventures and leadership programs in the Scandinavian wilderness. We don't know if we will ever write a follow-up book, but there will certainly be a follow-up journey. Our world trip and the people we have met have given us too much inspiration to sit still. We hope you find the same inspiration in our story and that you become motivated to travel, discover, try new things, leave your comfort zone, and overcome fear. We would love to hear about your victories, and you would help us tremendously by leaving a review after you have finished reading our story.

Leaving the Comfort Zone

The Adventure of a Lifetime

Text and photography by Olivier Van Herck and Zoë Agasi

Edited by Robert Klanten, Olivier Van Herck, and Zoë Agasi

Text editing by Tom Hill
Copyediting by Jennifer Fratianni

Editorial Management by Arndt Jasper

Design, layout, and cover by Melanie Ullrich
Layout assistance by Stefan Morgner

Photo Editor: Zoe Paterniani

Typefaces: FF Tisa Sans by Mitja Miklavčič
and Guyot by Ramiro Espinoza

Photo p. 236: Domcobb/Alamy Stock Photo
Maps: © Free Vector Maps, Striped Candy LLC

Printed by Printer Trento s.r.l., Trento, Italy
Made in Europe

Published by gestalten, Berlin 2023
ISBN 978-3-96704-098-2

For more information, and to order books, please visit www.gestalten.com

Bibliographic information published by the Deutsche Nationalbibliothek.
The Deutsche Nationalbibliothek lists this publication in the
Deutsche Nationalbibliografie; detailed bibliographic data is
available online at www.dnb.de

None of the content in this book was published in exchange for payment
by commercial parties or designers; the inclusion of all work is based
solely on its artistic merit.

This book was printed on paper certified
according to the standards of the FSC®.